The Ukulele

An Illustrated Workshop Manual

By Graham McDonald

MusicBooks Press

Published by MusicBooks Press
Graham McDonald Stringed Instruments
PO Box 365, Jamison
ACT 2614 Australia

First printed: 2019

ISBN: 978-0-9804762-9-3

Set (mostly) in 10pt *Myriad Regular* with the headings in *Paoul*

NATIONAL LIBRARY OF AUSTRALIA

A catalogue record for this book is available from the National Library of Australia

THE UKULELE

AN ILLUSTRATED WORKSHOP MANUAL

CONTENTS

THE PARTS OF A UKULELE

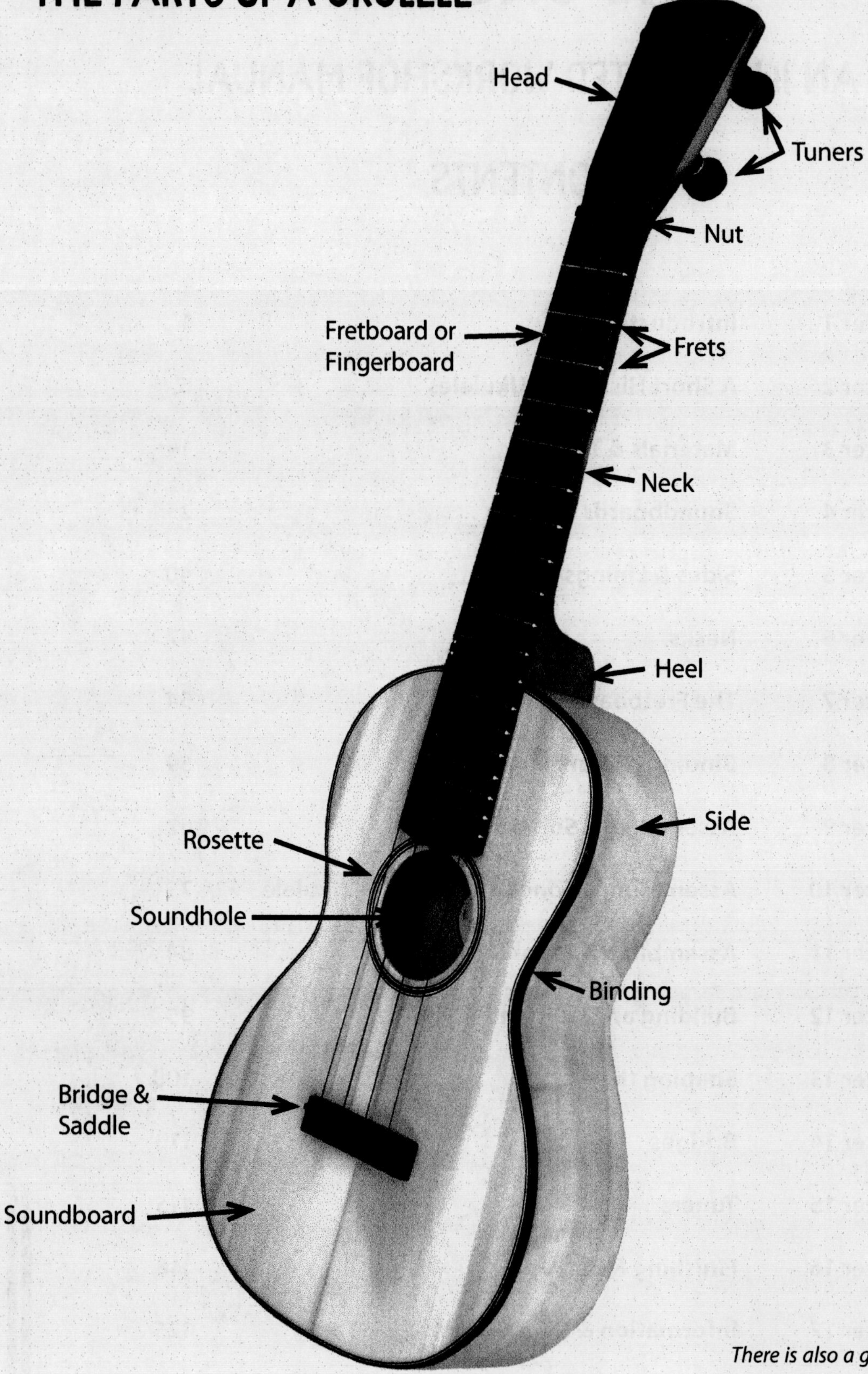

There is also a glossary of ukulele terminology on page 132.

FORWARD

This is my third 'how-to' book on building musical instruments, this one on ukuleles of various sizes. As with the two previous books, I have tried to avoid describing just one approach to the various processes involved in making the instruments, rather offering a variety of methodologies from which the user of the book may choose. This does mean that the user should read through the book first and think about how their ukulele is going to be constructed.

The book is aimed at people with some experience and understanding of woodworking who have a familiarity with using both hand and power tools. Some knowledge of how stringed musical instruments are built and the terminology used will be very useful. A glossary is included on page 144 to supplement the diagram on the opposite page.

For each process in building a ukulele I have tried to show a couple of alternate ways of doing it, but there are probably half dozen other ways any of the procedures described here can be done. Part of the continuing fascination with building stringed musical instruments that there is no one correct way to do any particular part of it. There are always alternatives and different approaches.

For various reasons, it has not been possible include full sized drawing of the ukuleles in the book. These are available as a download at *www.mcdonaldstrings.com/ukebook/UkulelePlans.pdf* These can be printed as required.

As with any such writing and publishing project there are many people to thank. First is my family and especially my ever patient wife Lynn who has stoically put up with these adventures for many years; our friends John and Mandy Doherty whose request for a ukulele to be made for their niece Julie started this whole ukulele journey; English ukulele maker Ken Timms whose documenting of his interpretation of the 1917 Ford Motor Co. film has been a great inspiration; Beau Hannam <beauhannamguitars.com>and Allen McFarlen of Barron River Guitars <brguitars.com> for the use of images of their ukuleles; Karl Neuenfeldt for his forensic proof-reading and suggestions; RM Mottola for his editing and comments and Scott Wise for his ever useful advice and ideas.

In memory of Graham Caldersmith, who helped so many of us to make better musical instruments.

CHAPTER 1
INTRODUCTION

This book covers the construction of the four common sizes of ukulele: soprano, concert, tenor and baritone. Differing construction techniques are used for the four instruments, with the idea that the book offers a 'cookbook' of different ways to build ukuleles which can be mixed and matched as required. This does mean that there is no simple linear description of building one ukulele, rather a series of chapters on fabricating the various parts; necks, soundboards, fretboards etc, followed by other chapters explaining how those parts are assembled into a finished instrument. This also means that a fair amount of pre-planing is required to determine what kind of ukulele is to be built, and how it is to be put together. Read through the book first and get an idea of what will be required in materials and tools as well as the various procedures to make a ukulele.

At its simplest, a ukulele can be assembled over a long weekend. At its most complex, the time necessary will be comparable to that needed for a fine classical or steel string guitar. Ukuleles are only limited by imagination.

One thing to remember is that there is not very much string tension on even the largest of ukuleles. As a comparison, a full sized classical guitar has a tension of over 38kg/86lb and a steel string guitar around 74kg/160lb. The soprano, concert and tenor all use the same re-entrant tuning G4-C4-E4-A4 (the famous My Dog Has Fleas) where the lowest note is the C4 at 261hz on the third string and the top A4 string at 440hz. During the first ukulele craze in the 19-teens and 20s the standard or soprano ukulele was often tuned a full tone higher to A4-D4-F#4-B4 with the strings at higher tension.

It is common on tenor size instruments for the G string to be tuned an octave lower - 'low G tuning' - and most of the string makers make sets to suit. The baritone tuning is D3-G3-B3-E4, the same as the top four strings of a guitar. The standard ukulele tuning keeps the same intervals between the strings (notwithstanding that the G4 string is an octave higher) as a guitar so the same chord shapes can be used, just transposed up a fourth.

UKULELE SIZES

This a table of general measurements for the four sizes of ukulele. These are not absolute and any of the measurements can vary by a couple of cm or an inch or so.

Size	**String length**	**String tension**	**Overall length**	**Body length**	**Body width**
Soprano	34cm/13.5"	10kg/22lb	53cm/21"	23cm/9"	17.5cm/7"
Concert	38cm/15"	15kg/33lb	55cm/22"	28cm/11"	20cm/8"
Tenor	43cm/17"	18kg/40lb	66cm/26"	30cm/12"	22cm/8.5"
Baritone	50cm/20"	24kg/53lb	76cm/30"	35cm/14"	25cm/10"

THE TYPES OF UKULELE

1. OLD ISLAND STYLE UKULELE

The earliest Hawaiian made ukuleles were tiny little instruments, made entirely of koa (*Acacia koa*). The frets were inset directly into the neck surface which was in the same plane as the soundboard. The tight waisted body shape was inherited from the Madieran machete and the construction methodology documented in a short film made in 1917 by the Ford Motor Company. This instrument is based on that film and made with Australian blackwood (*Acacia melanoxylon*), a close relative of koa. It uses a 34cm/13½" scale or string length.

2. THE SOPRANO UKULELE

The soprano ukulele is based on a Regal design which was made by the thousands in the 1920s and sold under a variety of labels. It is a simple ukulele, made as lightly as possible. Three of this style of ukulele were made during the writing of this book. Pictures of all three instruments have been used at various times.

The body was made separately from the neck and joined by a shallow violin-style mortice. A thin fretboard, made from ebony, with 12 frets, sits on top of the neck and slightly overhangs the body. The bridge is simply made with four holes drilled for the strings. Small glass beads are tied to the ends of the strings which lock them under the soundboard. This ukulele also has a 34cm/13½" scale.

3. THE CONCERT UKULELE

The concert is the second smallest size of ukulele, and perhaps the least common. The string length is two frets longer than the soprano, around a 38cm/15" scale length, and according to the string manufacturers around 50% more string tension. The concert size ukulele needs more bracing on the soundboard but the body can be built with the soundboard, back and sides the same thickness as the soprano, around 1.5mm/0.060". The body is a little longer, wider and deeper, and with the added string tension the sound produced should be louder and more resonant.

The shape of this instrument is based on a enlarged Martin soprano ukulele, following the Martin length, width and depth. Unlike the 'old island style' soprano, this instrument has a separate fretboard which can either be a short 12 fret style, or can be extended to the soundhole using 19 frets. The body and neck are made from Honduras mahogany (*Swietenia macrophylla*) with a rosewood fretboard and bridge.

The ukulele is built on a workboard or 'solera' in the manner of traditional classical guitar making. Using a flat workboard does simplify construction. The neck is glued to the soundboard with the sides let into slots cut into the end of the neck. The soundboard braces are flat, rather than arched as they might be on a guitar, with the neck in the same plane as the soundboard. The back is arched over braces and the sides shaped to a section of a spherical dome matching the curvature of the braces. This sounds complex, but is easily done with a dished workboard lined with sandpaper which both shapes the braces and sands the sides to the required profile.

Although the solera workboard method is only used for the concert and baritone ukuleles in this book, it is adaptable to any size ukulele. Because the workboards themselves are quite small it is simple and cheap enough to make one for each size of instrument. The moveable dowels which establish the body shape allow for variation in the body outline. A soprano ukulele in a Martin or Regal body design (as included in the plans) could be made on a slightly smaller solera workboard.

With this method of construction the actual assembly of the instrument takes very little time, but only after the constituent parts - neck, soundboard, back and sides - have been prepared.

4. THE TENOR UKULELES

The tenor ukulele has become very popular in recent years as a solo instrument. The longer 43cm/17″ scale means higher string tension with standard G4-C4-E4-A4 tuning. This should lead to a louder and more responsive instrument. Many players alternatively use a low G3 string which adds extra range to the instrument. The body design for the two tenor ukuleles built for this book is based on a Gibson L-00 guitar from the 1930s. For the first one the body and neck are made with mahogany and the soundboard is Californian redwood (*Sequoia sempervirens*), recycled from an old stair tread a century or more old. This ukulele is made with 12 frets to the neck/body join.

The body and neck are made separately and bolted together using a small threaded insert in the neck heel and a short M4 thread bolt. The back of the neck heel has a 18mm/¾″ wide tenon that extends 10mm/⅜″ into a mortice in the neck block which provides vertical alignment of the neck. The section of the fretboard over the body is supported by an extension of the neck the same width as the tenon.

The second instrument has 14 frets to the body with the body made from Australian red cedar (*Toona australis*), recycled from a piece of century old skirting board, with the neck from mahogany. This instrument uses a simpler bolt-on neck. A 14 fret to the body neck means that bridge position is closer to the soundhole and the soundboard bracing is adjusted slightly.

The bodies are constructed in a solid mould using solid rather than kerfed linings. There is a double layer of linings for the soundboard and a single lining strip for the back.

5. THE BARITONE UKULELE

The baritone ukulele is edging closer to a guitar, with a longer 50cm/20" string length with a usual tuning of D3-G3-B3-E4. That is the same as the top four strings on a guitar, albeit with a lower string tension due to the shorter scale. The assembly of this instrument is again done on a solera workboard in the Spanish style.

There is more bracing on the larger soundboard and back, with five fan braces on the soundboard and three transverse back braces. The lower transverse brace on the soundboard is slightly arched, around .75mm/ 0.030" drop from the centre to the edges. The slight arch on the lower part of the soundboard allows the larger baritone sized soundboard to move a little with humidity changes.

The soundboard is Sitka spruce (*Picea sitchensis*), the back and sides are tamarind (*Tamarindus indica)* and the neck Queensland maple (*Flindersia brayleyana*). The fretboard and bridge are made from Indian rosewood (*Dalbergia latifolia*).

Full sized drawings of all five ukuleles to accompany the book are available at www.mcdonaldstrings.com/ukebook/ukuleleplans.pdf

CHAPTER 2
A SHORT HISTORY OF UKULELES

The ukulele, as we know it, is less than a century and a half old. In the beginning there was the *cavaquinho*, a small four-string guitar from northern Portugal. Cavaquinhos spread to Brazil, the Azores, the East Indies and Madeira, a small Portuguese island off the coast of Morocco otherwise best known for its wine. On Madeira this little instrumens was known as a *machete*, sometimes *machete de braga* or *braguinha* (Braga is a northern Portuguese city known for woodworking). There was also a slightly larger five string instrument, the *rajao* with a string length of 42cm/16-17" compared to the 33cm/13" scale of the machete. The smaller machete was tuned in an open G tuning d-g-b-d while the larger rajao used a re-entrant tuning d-g-c-e-a with the middle c string the lowest pitch. The soundboards of both were a softwood, probably imported, but the bodies and necks used local hardwoods. Tourists to the island would often comment on the machete music that was part of the island's soundscape.

The machete and rajao arrived in Hawaii with a shipload of Madeiran immigrants in 1879 and within a few years the machete had become the *ukulele* and the rajao the *taropatch* or *taropatch fiddle*. They were being made entirely of koa (*Acacia koa*), a

One of the earliest photographs of a ukulele, held by the woman on the left, along with two other hula dancers holding a guitar (centre) and a rajao (on the right). The photo was taken around 1885 in James J. Williams' photographic studio in Honolulu. The original is in the Hawaii State Archives.

hardwood found only on the Hawaiian islands and much used for canoes and furniture. This was a time of re-emergence of Hawaiian language and tradition and the ukulele and taropatch were quickly adopted as parts of Hawaiian musical culture. The re-entrant tuning of the rajao was used for the ukulele, using the top four strings of the larger instrument in the familiar g-c-e-a tuning.

Three of the arrivals on that 1879 ship - Augusto Diaz, Manuel Nunes, and José do Espirito Santo - had set themselves up making furniture and various kinds of guitars. Within a few years they became the first manufacturers of the new ukulele. Apart from the use of koa, the early ukulele makers simplified the construction a little. A separate fretboard sitting on top of the neck and soundboard was abandoned for the frets being inserted directly into the neck itself, flush with the soundboard, suggesting that no-one could see any use for more than 12 frets. The machete's pin bridge was also set aside in favour of a simple bridge with four slots or holes cut in the back that would hold a knot tied in the gut strings.

By the early years of the new century the ukulele was becoming popular along the west coast of the US mainland with instruments imported from Hawaii and sold by distributors in both San Francisco and Los Angeles. Gradually the ukulele spread across the United States through vaudeville entertainers and other Hawaiian themed theatrical performances as well as the large trade and cultural expositions which were regularly held in major cities. By 1912 manufacturing had started on the mainland, with

The De Lano Steel Guitar and Ukulele Sextette of Los Angeles, featured in The Crescendo, September 1916. Charles De Lano was one of the earliest ukulele teachers and promoter on the US West Coast, offering ukulele lessons from 1912 and forming the first Ukulele Club in 1913. Image courtesy Gregg Miner.

Leonardo Nunes, the son of Manuel, setting up a factory in Los Angeles. In the autumn of 1914 the ukulele was listed in the Sears Roebuck catalog for the first time, a significant addition in that important barometer of music taste.

The breakthrough was the 1915 Panama Pacific International Exposition held in San Francisco. Lured into the Hawaiian pavilion by huge tanks of tropical fish, the crowds were entertained by a five-piece band playing Hawaiian music on guitars, a mandolin and a ukulele. That group, organised by ukulele builder Jonah Kumalae, was the hit of the Exposition and started a major craze for the ukulele which lasted for the next 15 years.

Within a year all the major music companies in Chicago and New York were producing ukuleles and the Hawaiian manufacturers could not keep up with demand. There are strong suggestions that Sears Roebuck bought the Harmony company of Chicago in 1916 to ensure a supply of ukuleles for their catalog sales. Up to that time ukuleles were most associated with Hawaiian music. The newfound popularity of

Three early koa wood ukuleles. On the left is a Kumalae No.22, made in Hawaii in the late 1920s. The body shape is typical of many of the early Hawaiian made ukuleles. In the centre is a Leonard Nunes, made in Los Angeles after 1916. On the right is a Washburn Style 1715, made in Chicago in the 1920s. Images courtesy ukulelecorner.co.uk, Kerry Char & John Bernunzio.

the instrument soon led to a form of quasi-Hawaiian popular music - *hapa-haole* (half white) - churned out by the popular song writers of the day. The songwriters soon found there was a market for a catchy refrain which mentioned one or more of Honolulu, Hawaii or ukulele. Soon ukulele chord diagrams began to appear on sheet music of popular songs and within a few years became an almost mandatory inclusion on any published music.

Initially there was only the standard soprano ukulele available. By the middle of 1917 the new *banjo-ukulele*, a small banjo body with a ukulele neck, was acclaimed as the 'novelty of the season' and was listed in the Sears Roebuck catalog by the Fall 1918 edition. Banjo-ukuleles, or *banjoleles* as they were sometimes called, became very popular in Britain through the late 1920s and 1930s, mostly because of their use by Music Hall comedian and movie star George Formby.

On the left is a top-of-the-line 1924 Martin 5K ukulele with an all-koa body and neck. In the centre is Gibson's fanciest ukulele, a Style 3 with a mahogany body probably from the late 1920s. On the right is a Harmony made Roy Smeck ukulele from 1929, with its curious 'seal' shaped soundholes. Images courtesy Retrofret, John Bernunzio & Retrofret.

The mass produced ukuleles of the 1920s and 30s depended on visual appeal rather than quality of construction. The Art Moderne model on the left and the stencilled palm tree ukulele in the middle were both made by Harmony in Chicago. The Art Moderne also features a pearloid fingerboard and head. On the right is a Le Domino, originally made by J.R. Stewart in Chicago and later by Regal. Painted all over in black with decals for the rosette and below the bridge. Images courtesy Retrofret.

In 1916 C.F. Martin & Co introduced a range of ukuleles and taropatches in three styles, designated 1, 2 and 3, in increasing levels of decoration. The taropatch had a larger body and longer 37.5cm/14.75" string length with four double courses of strings in ukulele tuning. In 1925 this size of instrument became the basis for the concert ukulele. This was joined in the catalogs a couple of years later by the tenor model with a slightly larger body than the concert and a 43cm/17" string length. Martin ukuleles were more expensive than most others, priced at $10, $15 and $25 in comparison to the Sears Roebuck ukuleles in 1917 which started at $2.45 up to their finest Koa wood instrument for $9.95. Martin raised the market another notch in 1921 with their all-Koa 5K model which retailed at $50.

The Great Depression of the late 1920s and 1930s brought the ukulele craze to a sudden finish amidst a major collapse of much of the American music industry. For the next 20 years the ukulele was relegated to Hawaii as tourist entertainment until a second round of enthusiasm arrived with television, the new plastics industry and an Italian jazz guitar maker. As television took over American lounge rooms in the late 1940s, it was the host of a TV variety and talent show, Arthur Godfrey, who sparked the revival of the ukulele, accompanying his own singing on his TV programs.

At the same time there were several entrepreneurs developing the idea of injection-moulded plastic musical instruments, including Mario Maccaferri. He had worked with Henri Selmer in the 1930s making the jazz guitars made famous by Django Reinhardt and had arrived in the United States in 1939. Maccaferri had developed plastic reeds for clarinets and saxophones during World War II

Three plastic Macaferri ukuleles from the 1950s. The purple TV Pal on the left has the bridge moulded as part of the soundboard. The red/yellow ukulele in the centre is the back of another TV Pal. The cream soundboard of the Islander DeLuxe on the right hides a swirling red body and neck. Images courtesy Retrofret and Ukester Brown.

On the left is a S.S. Stewart labeled banjo ukulele from around 1928 and on the right is a 1930 National Triolian resonator ukulele in their polychrome finish with a two colour stencilled palm-tree on the back. Both instruments have string lengths close to 38cm/15" which makes them effectively 'concert' size instruments. Images courtesy Retrofret.

when there was a shortage of natural cane for that purpose and was seeking other musical uses for the new injection moulding technology. He came up with a functional and good sounding ukulele modelled on the Martin Style 0, but moulded in eight parts. Godfrey promoted it on his TV show and Maccaferri sold millions of them, mostly as toys to the, then young, 'baby-boomer' generation..

Godfrey may also have been responsible for the development of the baritone ukulele around 1950. There are two competing stories about the baritone's emergence. One is that Godfrey asked a musician friend, banjoist Eddie Connors, to design a larger, lower pitched ukulele. These were then made and sold by Vega in Boston with Godfrey's name on the headstock. The alternative story is that the idea of the baritone came from the ukulele building family business of Favilla on Long Island, NY. Both made baritone ukuleles with 48cm/19" string lengths and it is quite possible that both came up with the idea independently around the same time.

Rock & Roll music and the electric guitar ended the second ukulele craze by the late 1950s, but it did leave the legacy of a generation of children who had their first musical experience of a strummed instrument on a ukulele. It was this generation who have re-embraced the ukulele in middle age as a vehicle for social music making. This has led to the current third revival of the ukulele which has included the rise of the modern artisan ukulele as well as the thousands of cheap ukuleles in every music shop.

This is only a brief outline of the story of the ukulele. Much more comprehensive accounts are contained in *The Ukulele - A History* by Jim Tranquada & John King (University of Hawai'i Press, 2012) and Jim Beloff's *The Ukulele - A Visual History* (Miller Freeman Books, 1997).

A 1950 Favilla baritone ukulele. Image courtesy Retrofret.

CHAPTER 3
MATERIALS & TOOLS

WOOD

Ukuleles can be made from the same timbers as other stringed instruments, such as guitars or violins. Unlike guitars and violins many ukuleles use hardwood soundboards, usually the same timber as the rest of the body and neck. This was traditionally Hawaiian koa (*Acacia koa*), a medium-weight timber native to Hawaii. Over-use of this wood in the past century has meant there is not much high-quality koa left. Supplies are limited and expensive.

The early 20th century alternative to koa was Central-American or Honduran mahogany (*Swietenia macrophylla*) but the same fate has befallen that timber and the sale of raw timber from Central American is restricted under the CITES (the Convention on International Trade in Endangered Species of Wild Fauna and Flora) treaty. Mahogany is plantation grown in Asia and some Pacific islands, so supplies are available and ukulele sized pieces should not be too hard to find.

There are other temperate and tropical hardwoods that can be used, such as monkeypod, mango, walnut and Australian blackwood (a close relative of koa). Specialist tonewood suppliers such as Luthiers Mercantile or Allied Lutherie have a bewildering array of timber available, and the relatively small sizes of the pieces needed for a ukulele can mean that even the most exotic can be purchased fairly inexpensively. This can also mean that interesting small pieces can often be found in a timberyard aimed at the furniture trade. A 14" bandsaw, the size commonly found in a lutherie workshop, is adequate to re-saw all the wood needed for a ukulele.

The early Hawaiian makers used koa because it was both available and highly valued in Hawaiian society. There has been, in recent years, an increased use of softwoods such as spruce for soundboards and both hardwood and softwood soundboards are equally acceptable.

The most important factor to consider when buying the timber needed for a ukulele is how it was sawn out of the log in the first place. Preferable is quarter-sawn timber, with the annular growth rings as close as possible to being perpendicular to the widest face of the board and the lengthways cuts following the grain of the wood. Wood can be imagined as a bundle of straws held together by the bark, and it is preferable for the sawing to take place as much as possible following the line of those straws. This isn't always practical or even possible as trees bend and twist as they grow and sawmillers will often have to compromise between end yield and the practicalities

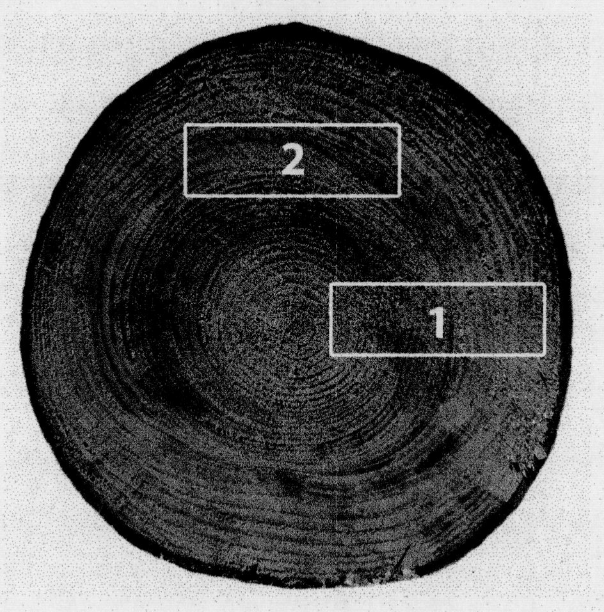

A newly cut softwood log. The section marked 1 is quarter-sawn, the section marked 2 is back- or slab-sawn.

of sawing. Quarter-sawing a log is the least efficient way of cutting it up, both in terms of the effort to do it and the amount of lumber produced at the end, but quarter-sawn timber is the most dimensionally stable as the timber is dried, and many, but not all, timbers show the most interesting figure in the wood on the quarter-sawn face.

The specialist tonewood suppliers will try to oversee the entire processing of the log, so what they sell is optimally cut for instrument use. Softwoods for the soundboard are often cut to appropriate lengths in the forest as the tree is felled and then the log sections are split into manageable billets and dried before being sliced into soundboards. The splitting means that it is easier to then do the final cutting with minimal 'runout'. On a perfect soundboard a sliver pulled off one corner would run the entire length of the soundboard. Most of the time little twists and irregularities in the tree means this won't happen, but a sliver should run several inches along an edge before tapering away to nothing. Less runout means that it will be easier to plane the soundboard, as bookmatched flat soundboard halves will have the runout going in opposite directions and planing across the centre join can get tricky.

Hardwoods would be more typically cut into 50mm-100mm/2-4" planks and dried before being re-sawn into thinner slices for backs and sides or blocks for neck stock. If the wood is being air dried, the general rule is a year per 25mm/1" of thickness, though kiln drying will accelerate this process. The difference between air- and kiln-dried wood is one of ongoing discussion in the stringed instrument world, but most people will admit that properly kiln dried timber is perfectly acceptable. The important thing is that it is dry and stable.

Wood purchased from a specialist tonewood supplier will usually be dry to a stable point where almost all the free moisture in the wood has gone, but the wood will still absorb and lose moisture depending on the local humidity levels. It is advisable to have any timber to be used in the workshop environment for a few weeks at least, so it matches the conditions in the workshop.

HUMIDITY CONTROL

Humidity, or at least the extremes of it, is the great enemy of stringed instruments. Wood absorbs and loses moisture continuously as the relative humidity changes and changes size as it does so. A thin, flat piece of wood, such as used for a soundboard or back will noticeably change in width going from the extremes of humidity. While this doesn't matter when it is just a flat piece of timber, once other bits of wood such as internal bracing are glued across the grain, the plate cannot contract and expand in the same way. The plate will still absorb and lose moisture, as will the braces, but the constriction of the bracing will mean that the plate will dome up as humidity increases, and flatten out as it decreases.

The small size of a ukulele means that the inbuilt soundboard doming is not as important as it might be on a guitar and the soprano, concert and tenor sizes can be made with flat soundboard braces. A 15' radius curve for the back braces is suggested. This curve is both practical and aesthetic. It means that even if the humidity falls to very low levels the plate won't go entirely concave and in very high humidity the dome is accentuated a little more.

A relative humidity of 40% is strongly suggested for all gluing of braces on flat soundboards and backs and for gluing the fingerboard to the neck. Cheap electronic humidity/temperature meters can be purchased at electronic suppliers which are accurate enough for this application and can be combined with a dial hygrometer and checking on-line weather reports. It is guaranteed that gluing soundboard or back braces in times of high humidity will be regretted.

What is most damaging to stringed instruments is sudden large changes in humidity and temperature. Gradual changes from one extreme to another can be coped with but rapid changes can be catastrophic with soundboards or backs literally cracking apart in extremely low humidity levels.

GLUES

Several different types of glue are used at various times in these instruments. For most gluing a PVA glue is used, either Franklin Titebond (the original formula, not the II or III version) or Luthiers Mercantile's Yellow Instrument Glue. Both of these set up much harder than the ordinary white PVA woodworkers glue commonly available in numerous brands. Titebond is an Aliphatic Resin Emulsion and of a yellowish colour, rather than the white colour of most PVAs, and has been the standard glue in the guitar building industry for many years. One thing to be careful about using these glues is that they don't work if the temperature is below 10°C/50°F. They dry to a white chalky consistency which is not very adhesive. Cleanup of any squeeze-out is important as residual dried glue can sit on the surface and be visible under a finish.

At the same time there are instrument makers who will only use hot hide glue. This glue has been used for centuries and is the standard glue of violin makers. It is a gelatine made from animal skins and requires dissolving in water and heating before use. While its adhesive qualities are excellent it is trickier to use than PVA with a relatively short 'open' time - the time available to get the two surfaces to be glued together and clamps applied. It is an excellent glue for gluing tentallones in place when assembled an integral neck ukulele. Cleanup can be simply done with a cloth and warm water.

Epoxy can be used for gluing the fretboard to the neck. One advantage of epoxy for this joint is that it does not add any moisture to the join, which can lead to a backbow to the fretboard. Cleanup must be done with acetone before the epoxy has cured. Both Stewart MacDonald and Luthiers Mercantile sell epoxies suitable for woodworking, and there are others available such as West Systems, Z-Poxy, Bob Smith, Devcon and NHP. A 30 minute cure time is suggested. Hobby shops specialising in radio controlled model aircraft are a useful source of these epoxies. Cheaper, hardware store or supermarket 5-minute cure epoxies are useful for gluing inlays into the head of an instrument, and can be coloured with wood dust to match the colour.

Cyanoacrylate glue, often called Super Glue or CA, is useful for gluing in fretboard markers or side position dots as well as repairs in ebony and rosewood when mixed with a little sanding dust. This glue comes in a variety of viscosities for different uses, but the cheap varieties available in supermarkets are fine for the uses mentioned above.

MEASUREMENTS

Most dimensions in the book are given in both metric and Imperial forms. Metric lengths are in centimetres or millimetres (*cm* and *mm*) and Imperial in fractions or decimal inches. When a meteric measurement has been converted to Imperial it will ofter err towards a slightly larger Imperial measurement.

Thin plates, such as soundboards, are usually given in decimal inches, eg. 0.060" rather than 1/16", which is almost, but not quite 0.060". (1mm is very close to 0.040") Sometimes only Inch fractions are used where there is a convention for that usage, such as saddle widths or drill sizes. A table of conversions is included in the Appendix.

MATERIALS REQUIRED

Sound board and back sizes are close to finished dimensions, with little allowance for any fault in the timber, such as end checks.The lengths for unbent sides allow at least 25mm/1" extra at each end to make the bending easier.

OLD STYLE ISLAND SOPRANO

What You Need

Soundboard: One piece of hardwood 25cm/10" long, 16.5cm/6½" wide, 3-5mm thick that will be reduced to 1.5mm/0.060" thick.

Back: One piece of hardwood 28cm/11" long, 16.5cm/6½" wide, 3-5mm thick that will be reduced to 1.5mm/0.060" thick. The extra length allows for the button glued to the base of the heel.

Sides: 2 pieces 40cm/16" long, 6cm/2⅜" wide, 1.5mm/0.060" thick.

Neck: One piece 6.5cm x 6.5cm x 35cm/ 2½" x 2½" x 14" for a neck cut out of a solid or laminated block. One piece 6.5cm x 2cm x 45cm/2½" x ¾" 18" for a built-up, scarf-joint neck.

Braces: 4 pieces 5mm x 10mm by 15cm/3/16" x 3/8" x 6" spruce.
Kerfed Linings: 4 pieces 5mm x 7mm x 40cm/3/16" x 9/32" x 16" ***or*** 6 x solid linings 2.5 x 7mm/3/32" x 9/32".
Tailblock: 6.5cm x 5cm x 15mm/2 3/8" x 2" x 5/8") laminated or solid hardwood or softwood.
Bridge: 6cm x 1.5cm x 8mm/2 3/8" x 5/8" x 5/16" hardwood, an off-cut from the neck can be used.

For the body and neck any light/medium timber used by guitar builders is suitable, including koa as well as mahogany, Australian blackwood, mango, monkeypod or other relatively light-weight and resonant hardwood.

CHICAGO STYLE SOPRANO

What You Need

Soundboard: One piece of hardwood 25cm/10"long, 17cm/6 3/4" wide 3-5mm thick that will be reduced to 1.5mm/0.060" thick. Two narrower book-matched pieces of timber could also be used for the soundboard and back.
Back: One piece of hardwood 25cm/10"long, 17cm/6 3/4" wide thicknessed to 1.5mm/0.060" thick (add 1.5cm/5/8" to the length if an integrated neck is used to allow for the heel cap).
Sides: 2 bookmatched pieces 40cm/16" long, 6cm/2 3/8" wide, 1.5mm/0.060" thick.
Neck: One piece of hardwood 6.5cm x 6.5cm x 35cm/2½" x 2½" x14" for a neck cut out of a solid or laminated block or one piece 6.5cm x 2cm x 45cm/2½"x ¾" x 18" for a built-up, scarf-joint neck.
Fretboard: 23cm/9" long x 5cm/2" wide x 4mm/0.160" thick hardwood. Ebony or rosewood are often used on more expensive instruments.
Braces: 4 pieces 5mm x 10mm x 15cm/3/16" x 3/8" x 6" spruce.
Kerfed Linings: 4 pieces 5mm x 7mm x 40cm/3/16" x 9/32" x 16"long ***or*** 6 x solid linings 2.5 x 7mm/3/32" x 9/32".
Neckblock: 5cm x 5cm x 18mm/2" x 2" x ¾".
Tailblock: 6cm x 5cm x 12mm/2 3/8" x 2" x ½" laminated or solid hardwood or softwood.
Bridge: 6cm x 1.5cm x 8mm/2 3/8" x 5/8" x 5/16" hardwood, an offcut from the neck can be used.

Most soprano ukuleles were originally made entirely from light/medium density hardwoods such as koa (*acacia koa*, a native Hawaiian hardwood) or mahogany. More recently other timbers such as Australian blackwood, mango or monkeypod have been used. Alternatively a softwood, such as spruce, Western Red cedar or redwood may be used for soundboards. The softwoods should be used a little thicker than a hardwood, perhaps 1.75mm/0.070" for spruce and 2mm/0.080" for cedar or redwood.

CONCERT

What You Need

Soundboard: 2 bookmatched pieces 32cm/13" long, 11cm/4½" wide, 3-5mm thick (or one piece 20cm/8" wide with a final thickness of 1.5mm/0.060").
Back: 2 bookmatched pieces 32cm/13" long, 11cm/4½" wide, 3-5mm thick (or one piece 20cm/8" wide) with a final thickness of 1.5mm/0.060".
Sides: 2 bookmatched pieces 50cm/20" long, 7cm/2 5/8" wide, 1.5mm/0.060" thick.
Neck: One piece of hardwood 6.5cm x 6.5cm x 35cm/2½" x 2½" x 14" or a piece 6.5cm x 2cm x 45cm/2½"x ¾" x 18" for a built-up, scarf-joint nec.
Fretboard: 28cm/11" long by 5cm/2" wide by 4mm/0.160" thick hardwood (ebony or rosewood suggested).
Braces: 8 pieces 5mm x 10mm by 15cm/3/16" x 3/8" x 6" spruce.
Kerfed Linings: 4 pieces 5mm x 7mm x 50cm/3/16" x 9/32" x 20" long ***or*** 6 x solid linings 2.5 x 7mm/3/32" x 9/32".
Tailblock: 6.5cm x 5cm x 12mm/2 5/8" x 2" x ½" laminated softwood or hardwood.
Bridge: 6cm x 1.5cm x 8mm/2 3/8" x 5/8" x 5/16" hardwood, an offcut from the neck.

Many concert size ukuleles are made with hardwood soundboards in the usual manner of a soprano. Alternatively a softwood, such as spruce, Western Red cedar or redwood may be used. The softwoods should be used a little thicker than a hardwood, perhaps 1.75mm/0.070" for spruce and 2mm/0.080" for cedar or redwood. For the body and neck many timbers used by guitar builders are suitable, including koa, mahogany, Australian blackwood, mango, monkeypod or other relatively light-weight and resonant hardwood.

TENOR

What You Need

Soundboard: 2 bookmatched pieces 35cm/14″ long, 12.5cm/5″ wide, 3-5mm thick (for ease of joining), with a final thickness of 1.75mm/0.070″.

Back: 2 bookmatched pieces 35cm/14″ long, 12.5cm/5″ wide, 3-5mm thick, final thickness 1.75mm/0.070″.

Sides: 2 bookmatched pieces 52cm/21″ long, 7.5cm/3″ wide, 1.5-2mm/0.060-0.080″ thick.

Neck: A piece of hardwood 6.5cm x 6.5cm x 40cm/2½″ x 2½″ x 16″ if cut from a solid block or a piece 6.5cm x 2cm x 57cm/2½″x ¾″ x 22½″ for a built-up scarf-joint neck.

Fretboard: 30cm/12″ long by 5cm/2″ wide by 4mm/0.160″ thick hardwood (ebony or rosewood suggested).

Braces: 8 pieces 5mm x 10mm by 20cm/3⁄16″ x 3⁄8″ x 8″) spruce.

Kerfed Linings: 4 pieces 5mm x 7mm x 52cm/3⁄16″ x 9⁄32″ x 21″ long ***or*** 6 x solid linings 2.5 x 7mm/3⁄32″ x 9⁄32″.

Neckblock: 25mm thick x 62mm high x 50mm wide/1″ x 2½″ x 2″ mahogany (or similar) with the grain in the same direction as the sides. This is for a separate bolt-on neck.

Tailblock: 7cm x 5cm x 15mm/2¾″ x 2″ x 5⁄8″ laminated or solid softwood or hardwood.

Bridge: 10cm x 2.5cm x 10mm/4″ x 1″ x 3⁄8″ hardwood, often rosewood or ebony.

Like concert size ukuleles, tenor and baritone size instruments can made with hardwood soundboards in the same manner as smaller instruments or a softwood, such as spruce, Western Red cedar or redwood, may be used. The softwoods should be used a little thicker again than a hardwood, perhaps 2mm/0.080″ for spruce and 2.25mm/0.090″ for cedar or redwood. For the body and neck just about any timber used by guitar builders is suitable.

BARITONE

What You Need

Soundboard: 2 book matched pieces 40cm/16″ long, 15cm/6″ wide, 3-5mm thick, to be reduced a final thickness of 2mm/0.080″.

Back: 2 bookmatched pieces 40cm/16″ long, 15cm/6″ wide, 3-5mm thick to be reduced a final thickness of 2mm/0.080″.

Sides: 2 bookmatched pieces 58cm/23″ long, 10cm/4″ wide, 1.5-2mm/0.060-0.080 thick.

Neck: One piece (solid or laminated) hardwood 6.5cm x 8cm x 45cm /2½″ x 3¼″ x 18″ or a piece 6.5cm x 2cm x 60cm /2½″x ¾″ x 24″ for a built-up scarf-joint neck.

Fretboard: 40cm/16″ long by 5cm/2″ wide by 4mm/0.160″ thick hardwood (ebony or rosewood suggested).

Braces: 12 pieces 5mm x 10mm by 30cm/3⁄16″ x 3⁄8″ x 12″ spruce.

Kerfed Linings: 4 pieces 5mm x 7mm x 58cm/3⁄16″ x 9⁄32″ x 23″ long ***or*** 6 x solid linings 2.5 x 7mm/3⁄32″ x 9⁄32″.

Tailblock: 9cm x 5cm x 15mm/3⅝″ x 2″ x 5⁄8″ laminated or solid softwood or hardwood.

Bridge: 10cm x 2.5cm x 10mm/4″ x 1″ x 3⁄8″ hardwood, often rosewood or ebony.

NOTE: For all sizes of ukulele wherever possible all timber should be quarter sawn. Kerfed linings, in larger size for guitars or smaller for ukuleles, are available from most lutherie supply shops.

TOOLS

Most of the tools listed below will be standard in a woodworker's workshop, but there will be some specialised instrument building tools as well.

STATIONARY POWER TOOLS

Bandsaw - a 14" saw will allow the preparation of parts for just about any ukulele. A ¼" wide, 6 tooth per inch is a good general purpose blade with wider blades commonly used for resawing.
Drill press - a mid-size bench mounted model with a ½" chuck and a selection of standard twist, brad point and Forstner bits. A useful addition is a Safe-T-Planer (originally made by Wagner, but now by Stewart MacDonald) which is useful for thicknessing pegheads.
Disk sander - a 8-12" disk sander.
1HP+ router mounted on a dedicated router table.
Wide belt drum sander - for ukuleles a small model with a 10" wide drum could be used, but larger sizes can be more versatile.
Useful but not essential...
Oscillating spindle sander
Thickness planer - such as a 12" Delta or similar
Jointer - a 6-8" model with a reasonably long bed
Small table saw with a .023" kerf fret slotting blade.

SMALL POWER TOOLS

Electric drill, mains powered.
Drill/driver, battery powered.
Laminate trimmer for binding jig.
Orbital sander, for backs and soundboards.
Dremel, or similar, with various accessories.

HAND TOOLS AND OTHER USEFUL THINGS

Hygrometer and possibly, depending on your climate, a humidifier or de-humidifier
(target is 40% relative humidity)
Clamps - you can never have too many
- 6-8 small cam clamps
- 4 large cam clamps
- an assortment of G and F clamps or you might know them as C and bar clamps
- several dozen spring clamps for kerfing (wooden clothes pegs or small plastic type)
- spool clamps made from threaded ¼" metal rod (or bolts) with discs of wood or polypropylene cutting board material. The clamping surfaces of wood discs should be covered in thin cork sheet.

Bench vice - preferably a Versa-Vice or Parrot vice which can rotate
Chisels - a range from ⅛" - 1"
Planes - a long shooting plane for joining plates, a smoothing plane, a block plane (a Veritas apron plane is a useful one)
Cabinet scrapers: straight and curved
Sharpening stones and honing guide
Cork sanding blocks
Machinist's square
Sliding bevel
Screwdrivers
Bradawl
Plastic compass for determining angles
Saws - razor saw, fretting saw, jewellers saw (for inlay)
Exacto knife or violin makers knives
Files: smooth mill file for fret levelling
Fretting hammer
Wood rasp, Surform or Microplane rasp, spokeshave for neck carving
Rulers - 6", 12" and a longer one, preferably in both imperial and metric that will allow measurements of 1/100" and 1/10 mm for fret placement
Dial caliper for measuring thickness of soundboards, back and sides
Fret cutters (flat-head nippers)

A shop-made spool clamp from a 3" x ¼" bolt with the discs cut from a polyethylene chopping board with a 1½" hole cutter.

LUTHERIE SPECIFIC TOOLS

Purfling cutter for binding ledges such as the Ibex Purfling Cutter or the Schneider gramil
Fret crowning file
Nut slotting files
Violin peg reamer (1:30 taper)

CONSUMABLES

Glues

wood glue (Titebond or LMI yellow glue) and/or hot hide glue
cyanoacrylate (superglue)
Weldbond 16 (or similar solvent based cement) glue for plastic binding
epoxy: a good quality 30 minute epoxy for fretboard gluing, a finishing resin for sealing/grain filling and a hardware store '5 minute' for inlays

Masking tape for binding
Sandpapers: 80, 120, 180, 240-grit aluminium oxide and 400-grit up to as fine as you want wet & dry paper for frets and finishing
Finishing and buffing materials (see the chapter on finishing for options)
Plywood, acrylic sheet, cork sheet, leather and wood for clamping cauls, templates and the like

Three different purfling/binding cutters. A Schneider gramil, an Ibex purfling cutter and a shop made version from scrap maple and an old chisel blade.

BUILDING FORMS

The ukuleles in this book are built on a variety of forms which are described in each chapter. The 'old island style' soprano ukulele uses an inside form on a base plate with rope and wedges holding everything in place. This is a now almost forgotten methodology documented in a 1917 film made by the Ford Motor Co. Modern soprano ukuleles are more often built using either of the two building forms described below.

The concert and baritone size instruments use a workboard in the style of a classical guitar solera, where the instrument is assembled face down on the workboard with the sides glued into slots cut into the neck itself. Workboards for soprano and tenor models can be made in the same way, adjusting the size as required.

CONCERT

The workboard starts off as a piece of 18mm/¾" plywood 51cm/21" long and 26cm/10½" wide. This is long enough for the body, the clamping caul for the tailblock and ending a few mm before the nut. Draw a centreline and trace the body outline, with the tail end of the body starting 35mm/1½" from the end. Trace a line around the outline that is 35mm/1½" outside it. Mark the neck support, from the end of the body, 5cm/2" wide and cut out the shape. The neck

A solera workboard for a concert size ukulele.

support extension should end 1cm/½" or so before the nut. Sand the cut end smooth and mark the centreline on the sanded face. This is used to align the neck when it is glued to the soundboard.

A tailblock clamping caul can be made from plywood or solid timber. It is 5cm/2" wide, 6cm/2⅜" high and thick enough that two ¼" hanger bolts can be inserted in the bottom to hold it firmly to the workboard with wing-nuts. The hanger bolts should be fixed at 2.5-3cm/1-1¼" centres and two slots cut from the end of the workboard to match. One side needs to be shaped to the curve of the tail and a notch cut in the bottom to clear the overhang of the soundboard.

To hold the sides to the planned shape, 6cm/2⅜" lengths of 3cm/1¼" dowel are also clamped to the workboard with hanger bolts and wing-nuts. At least three on each side are needed, but five can give more control over the final shape. Individually shaped blocks could be used, but the large dowels can be used anywhere around the perimeter, just touching the side at one point. Again, a notch is taken out on one side at the bottom, to clear the soundboard overhang.

A 15mm/⅝"hole is drilled is drilled on the centreline of the workboard in the middle of where the soundhole will be. It is that diameter to take a short length of metal curtain rod which acts as an axle for a sandpaper lined dished workboard that will be used to shape the sides to the body taper and the arched back braces. The axle and relevant hole can of course be whatever size and material is convenient and available.

Two pieces of timber (5 x 2.5cm/ 2"x1" pine is fine) are attached to the underneath of the workboard. These support the workboard off the surface of a workbench or allow the workboard to be clamped in a vice. One piece is placed lengthways and secured by two countersunk screws from the top. It needs to be short enough to clear the wing-nuts for the tailblock caul and stop halfway along the neck. The second is notched over the top of the first across the widest part of the body and similarly screwed into place.

A ¼" or M6 thread T-nut can be fitted into the lengthways piece of timber in the centre of the hole drilled for the sanding disk axle. The photo of a workboard on the previous page shows an alternative approach with the T-nut hole in front of the axle hole and the T-nut mounted in the underside of the workboard itself. A bolt fitted to the T-nut can hold down the soundboard firmly to the workboard using a simple clamping system across the two transverse braces. The bottom photo on page 80 shows such a clamping system. It MUST be removed before the back is glued in place.

An optional addition is to fix a number of wood screws around the edge that can act as anchors for large rubber bands which can be used to clamp the back in place for gluing.

BARITONE

The solera workboard for the baritone ukulele is 60cm/24" long and 32cm/12½" wide. The tailblock caul is 8.5cm/3⅜" high and 5cm/2" wide. There are six other slots on each side for dowel side supports.

BODY MOULDS

The bodies of the tenor and the Chicago style soprano ukulele are constructed separately from the neck in an outside mould in the way commonly used for constructing steel string guitars. The neck is then attached to the body using a small bolt and a threaded insert fitted to the neck heel or set into a mortice in the neck block.

The mould is constructed in two halves and bolted together at each end. Two blocks are made by glue- laminating three or four pieces of plywood or MDF (or a combination of the two). The blocks need to be about 6cm/2⅜" thick - the height of the neck block. This might depend on the thickness of the materials available, the one used here was made from layers of 15mm plywood on the outside sandwiching two layers of 16mm MDF. The blocks are as long as the ukulele body plus 5cm/2" on each end and half the total body width plus 2.5cm/1" wide. For the tenor ukulele the initial size of the blocks was 14cm/5½" x 40cm/16". The corners are cut away to facilitate clamps that might be needed to hold the shoulders of the body outline firmly into the mould shape.

A 'spreader' at the waist is made from two layers of the plywood which are cut to the inside line of the waist. Two short pieces of threaded rod and four wing-nuts keep the spreader blocks in contact with the mould. The rectangular extensions at each end are cut squarely to allow a hole for a ¼" bolt to be drilled. These extensions are also a solid clamping caul for gluing the neck and tail blocks.

For the smaller soprano ukulele the two laminated blocks started out 10cm x 33cm/4" x 13" and 4.5cm/1⅞" thick.

The external shape should be cut and the two blocks bolted together before the body outline is marked on the top surface. The halves can then be un-bolted and the inside waste cut out on a bandsaw.

The shape can be refined with sanding drums or a spindle sander making sure to keep the inside shape square to the top surface.

Of course, any of the four sizes of ukulele can be made with any of these approaches, though the small size of a soprano instrument makes the bolt-on neck a little more fiddly to accomplish.

If a radiused sanding dish is used (as described on the next page) with a solid mould, a base plate will be needed to hold the mould and provide a location for an axle for the dish to rotate around. A piece of MDF is all that is needed with a couple of bolts to secure the mould and a hole drilled on the centreline for the axle. The Auxiliary Workboard described on page 24 can be used for this and other uses.

Laminating layers of plywood and MDF for a body mould.

The finished mould with the two halves held together with ¼" bolts.

Cutting the body shape out of a mould half.

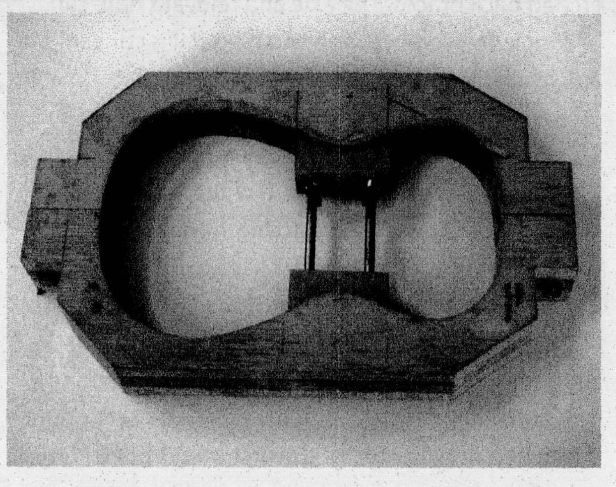

A mould for a soprano ukulele with waist spreader blocks fitted.

RADIUSED DISHED WORKBOARDS.

These workboards are used for both gluing the back braces to a ukulele back and, when lined with coarse sandpaper, to shape the sides and blocks into a small section of a sphere. These are available commercially in a number of different radii, usually designed for guitar building use, but it is a simple and cheap device to build. A 15′ radius is suggested for the back of a ukulele, but a tighter, 12′, radius could also be used. Materials needed are two pieces of MDF or plywood 50cm/18″ square, one 18mm/¾″ thick and the other 3mm/⅛″ thick as well as twelve pieces of dressed 50x25mm/2x1″ pine that are around 21.5cm/8½″ long.

Gluing the first two curved strips.

Drill a ¼″ hole in the middle of both pieces of the MDF/ply and cut a 45cm/18″ diameter circle. A piece of wood with a ¼″ hole at one end and another 22.5cm/9″ away to take a pencil makes a simple compass. Using the 15′ radius pattern in the downloaded plans, cut curved strips from the lengths of 2″x1″ pine. The pieces should end up 5mm/3⁄16″ thick at one end and 10mm/⅜″ thick at the other. Glue the first two so they butt together in the middle, and add the others, shortening them as required. Once all are in place sand any unevenness out and glue on the piece of 3mm MDF/ply, using a short length of ¼″ dowel as an alignment pin through the centres. The best way to apply pressure is with go-bars in a go-bar cabinet. This is simply a rigid structure with a floor and ceiling and lengths of dowel the same length as the distance between floor and ceiling. Suppliers offer wood or fibreglass bars 24″ in length, though longer ones are not a problem. Those shown are 105cm/42″ in length and made from 10mm/⅜″ dowel.

Gluing strips three and four. These are trimmed shorter to meet the first two strips.

The hole in the centre should be enlarged to whatever size dowel or metal tubing there is available to use as an axle. In this case a short length of 15mm/⅝″ metal curtain rod was used. The inside surface can be covered with strips of 60- or 80-grit sandpaper glued in place with contact cement. A knob or handle can be fixed to the back to help rotate the dish. It could also be mounted on a more permanent axle with the sandpaper side facing up and rotated by an electric motor in the manner of a potter's wheel.

Gluing strips five to eight. These have been shaped to fit between the first four.

Marking the final four strips to fit.

All twelve strips glued in place.

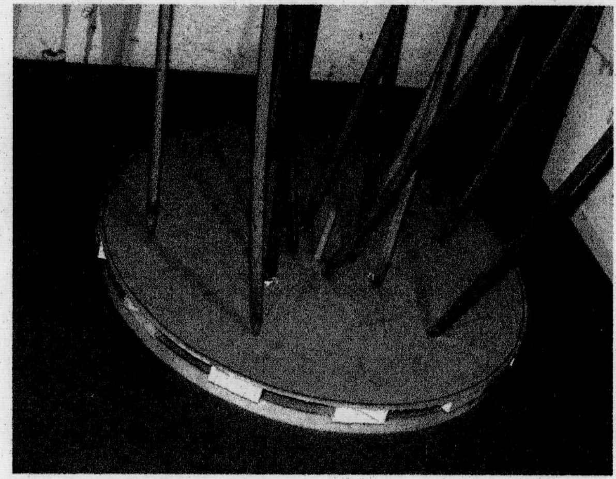

The 3mm/⅛" MDF top plate glued into place in a go-bar deck.

AUXILIARY WORKBOARD

A useful addition is a workboard that can be mounted in a vice, especially one that rotates, and used for jobs such as brace carving where it is good to be able to get at the work from several angles. Holes can be drilled in the workboard for specific tools like circle cutters and radiused sanding disks. The one used here is 35cm/14" x 50cm/19" and made from a piece of 18mm/¾" marine ply screwed to a length of 10cm/4"x 5cm/2" hardwood 50cm/19" long, but they can be made to any convenient size.

Other pieces of plywood or melamine coated MDF can be used as flat sanding boards. A sanding board cut to the size of half a sheet of sandpaper (cut lengthwise) is useful for many jobs and a larger sanding board, the size of up to four sheets of sandpaper can be used for flattening neck blanks or levelling linings on the inside of the ukulele body.

Full sized drawings of all five ukuleles to accompany the book are available at www.mcdonaldstrings.com/ ukebook/ukuleleplans.pdf

CHAPTER 4
SOUNDBOARDS & BACKS

SOUNDBOARDS

The soundboards of all ukuleles are made in much the same way. They are flat sheets of wood, made from a single piece or two pieces glued together and thinned to between 1.5-2mm/0.060-0.080" thick. They are usually cut into a small figure-of-eight guitar shape, although there are many ukuleles with alternative shapes. A soundhole is cut around a third of the way from the top end and a bridge glued around two-thirds the distance to the end of the body. The soundboard can be made from the same hardwood as the rest of the instrument or one of the commonly used softwoods can be substituted.

On the inside of the soundboard are a number of softwood re-enforcements or 'braces' which add stiffness to offset the tension of the strings and determine the tonal quality of the ukulele. These braces get larger and more numerous as the string tension increases in the larger sizes.

There is no acoustic difference between a one-or two-piece soundboard. It is a matter of what wood is available and the aesthetics of the design. The wood selected should be quarter-sawn, especially if using a softwood.

The small soprano ukulele with a body only 15cm/6" wide is often made with a single piece of timber each for the soundboard and back. Larger types of ukulele more often use two 'book-matched' pieces of timber, veneers cut sequentially from a thicker board so the grain patterns show a mirror image on each side of the centre join.

A TWO PIECE SOUNDBOARD OR BACK

The two pieces to be joined should be obtained or cut around 5mm/0.200" thick. Before joining they should be planed or sanded to no less than 3.5mm/0.140". Having the soundboard halves an even thickness and smooth makes the centre joining process a little easier.

This join must be made as accurately as possible as the soundboard and back will be reduced in thickness to no-more than 2mm/0.080" or less. Any imperfection in the joint can lead to a catastrophic and embarrassing failure of the glue line.

The traditional method of edge joining two thin slices of timber uses a long jointing plane and a simple jig to hold the timber perpendicular to the blade. The cutting edge of the blade needs to be perfectly straight, rather than slightly curved as smoothing planes sometimes are, and parallel to the

Planing the centre join of a soundboard half using a long plane and a shooting board.

sole of the plane. This will ensure a perfectly straight edge on both pieces of wood. When the planed edges are held together before a bright light no glimmer should be visible between them. If a jointing plane is not available, a shorter plane may be used, but the perfect join may be harder to accomplish. A sanded joint is possible, using the planing jig and a straight edge such as the side of a carpenter's level with 120-grit sandpaper stuck to it.

There are several ways to glue and clamp the soundboard and back. The simplest method is a simple jig to wedge them together. A piece of melamine covered MDF a little larger that the finished plate is required. A batten is attached to one edge, with another that can be clamped on the other side. As shown in the picture below, the two halves are placed on the fixture on top of a sheet of baking or waxed paper with the open join supported by a third batten of 13mm/½" thick material (plywood or solid timber). The second batten is clamped firmly in position. Glue is applied to the edges, the supporting batten is removed and the two pieces pushed flat. The third batten is then clamped on top of the join over another piece of baking/waxed paper. Alternatively a couple of bricks or other weights can be used to hold everything down while the glue dries overnight.

It is useful to offset the ends of the pieces by a couple of mm as a visual reference to the centre join. A well executed joint can just about disappear in some timbers, especially softwoods.

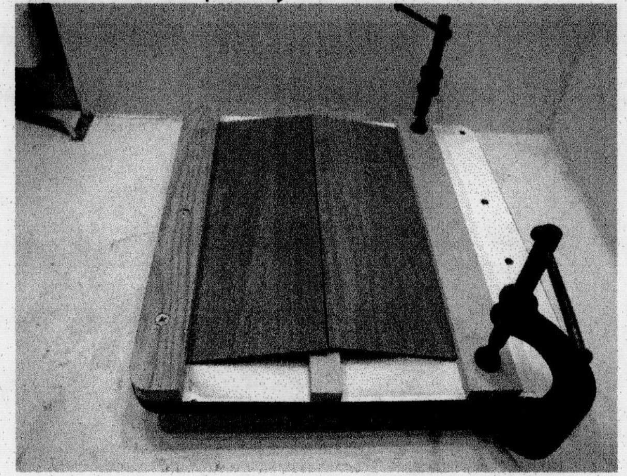

Two soundboard or back halves ready for gluing.

The two halves glued and clamped. Greaseproof or waxed paper is used to prevent the glued join sticking to the jig.

A slightly more complex alternative is the traditional Spanish method using battens, rope and wedges. The pieces to be joined are placed on three battens made of 50x25mm/2x1" timber, with another three laid on top. The battens should be long enough to overhang each end by 3-4cm/1½". Rope is then looped around the battens reasonably tightly in a figure-of-eight pattern and tied off. Wedges, cut from the same size timber, are inserted between the top battens and the rope to tighten everything up. The pictures show the stages of looping the rope around the battens. A couple of dry runs before doing it with glue will assist with getting the process done quickly and smoothly. Candle wax rubbed onto the middle of the battens will help stop then becoming glued to the joined plates as well.

The parts of the Spanish rope and wedges gluing fixture.

The base ready for the two halves.

A loop at the end of the rope allows it to be securely fixed at one end and the first figure-of-eight loop is in place around the end battens.

The two halves placed on the base with the centre join slightly offset.

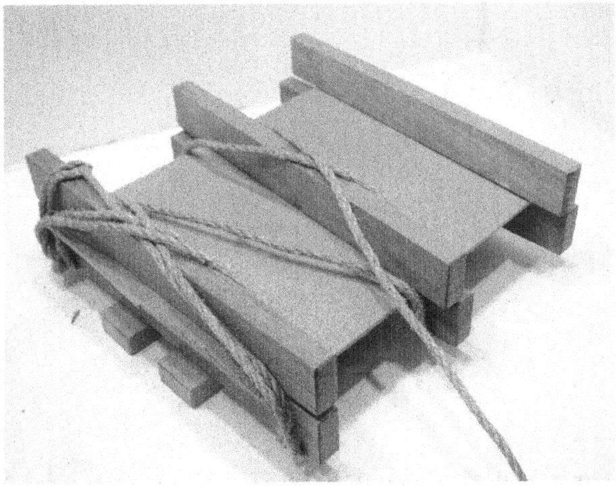

The second figure-of-eight on the end battens and the first on the centre battens.

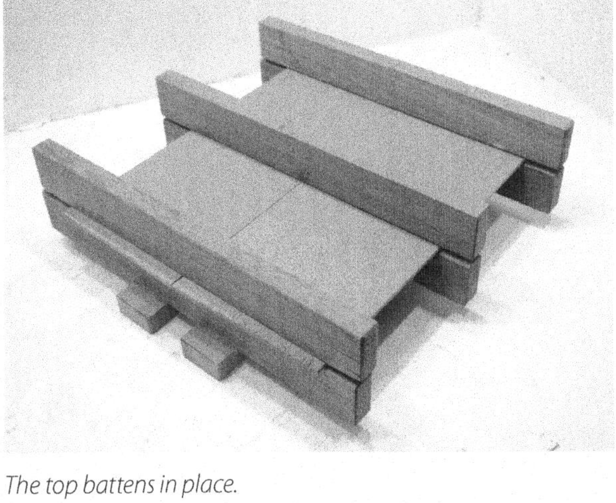

The top battens in place.

The first loop around the third set of battens.

The final loops around the third battens and the rope is tied off.

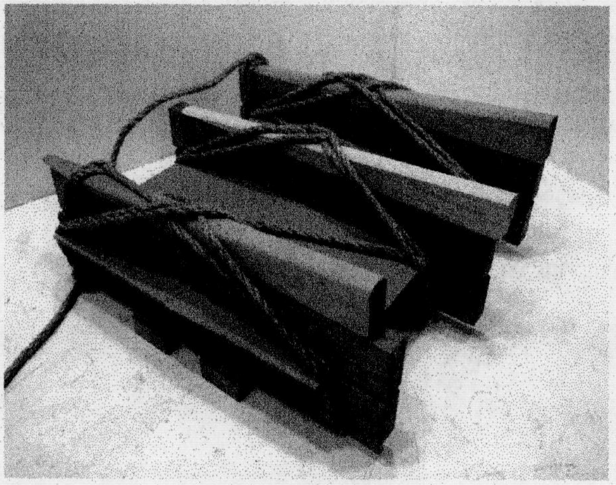

The wedges inserted to pull the join tight.

Leave the joined plates at least overnight before any final thicknessing. Whether using hide glue or an aliphatic resin, moisture is absorbed into the wood and it swells slightly. Planing or sanding to final thickness before that moisture has left the wood can lead to a noticeable dip along the join a day or so later.

If a rosette is to be inlaid in the soundboard, reduce the thickness to no less than 3-4mm/0.120"-0.160". If no rosette is used the soundboard (or the back) can be reduced to final thickness. Mark the position of the braces and the bridge plate on the inside as shown in the plans.

ROSETTES

A rosette in the soundboard around the soundhole is mostly a decorative element, but it does add a little extra strength and rigidity around the soundhole. The rosette can be as simple as a couple of concentric lines of purfling, while more complex designs might use the same materials as the binding or something more fanciful. A jig of some kind will be required to cut a channel or channels around 1.5mm/0.060" deep in the soundboard that is just a little wider than whatever is to be inlaid. The channel should be cut .25mm/0.010" larger than the calculated total width of the rosette elements. As soon as glue is applied everything will swell a little, and a push-fit without glue can suddenly be much tighter.

A fly-cutter in a drill press at a slow speed can be used to cut the channel, making sure that a depth-stop controls the depth of the cut. An MDF or ply-wood base should be fixed to the table of the drill press with a hole to accept the guide bit of the cutter. The soundboard should be clamped to the base and the depth-stop set. A fly-cutter with two blades can cut both the inner and outer lines of a rosette with the waste carefully chiseled away. Once the rosette

A rosette made from maple and Peruvian walnut rope binding with maple veneer borders.

is completed and the soundboard reduced to final thickness the fly-cutter can then be used to cut the soundhole.

There are jigs for a Dremel miniature router (or one of the similar machines on the market) that are specifically designed for this job. The Stewart-MacDonald Soundhole and Rosette Routing Jig and their Precision Router Base, used to have a minimum cutting diameter of 3″/7.5cm, but the recent interest in ukulele building has seen this modified so it is now adjustable down to a 2″ diameter cut. Older models

Extra mounting holes drilled and hole for bit clearance extended on an older model Stewart-MacDonald circle and rosette cutting jig for a Dremel Moto-tool.

The Dremel baseplate fitted to the rosette cutting jig to allow a smaller diameter circle to be cut, such as that on a soprano ukulele.

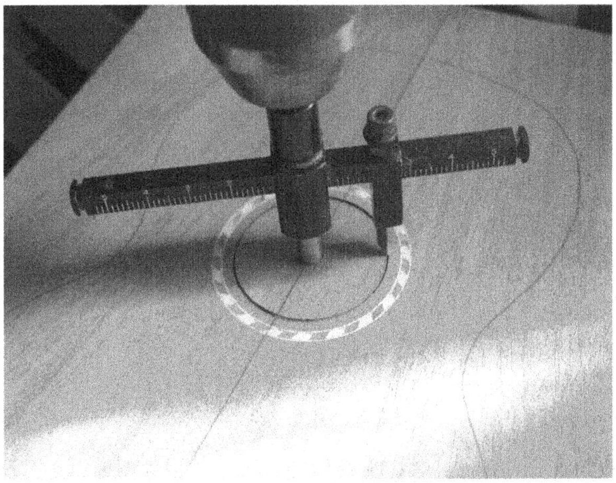
Using a fly-cutter to cut out a soundhole. The same tool can be used to cut two shallow concentric circles into the soundboard and the waste chiseled out for an inlaid rosette.

need modification to allow smaller diameter rosette channels and soundholes to be cut. The photos show one way this can be done.

The tenor ukulele uses the same tortoise-shell celluloid and B/W purfling for the rosette as well as the binding. A 5mm/3/16″ strip of celluloid binding is carefully cut in half down the middle and the two pieces used side by side as the centre of the rosette, edged by a strip of B/W fibre purfling.

A rosette made from two pieces of tortoise-shell celluloid binding bordered by black/white purfling strips matching the binding and purfling around the edge of the soundboard.

Two bookmatched offcuts from the tamarind baritone ukulele back are glued together and then the centre is glued to a scrap plywood base.

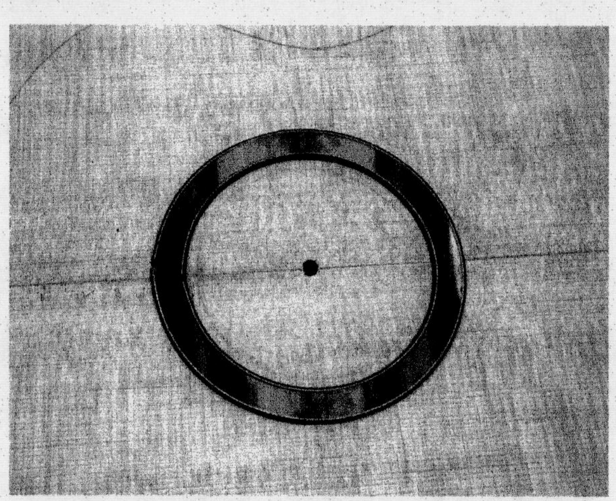

A disc is cut from the offcuts 8-10mm/5⁄16-3⁄8" wide and a 1mm deep channel cut in the soundboard, wide enough to allow the disc and purfling borders.

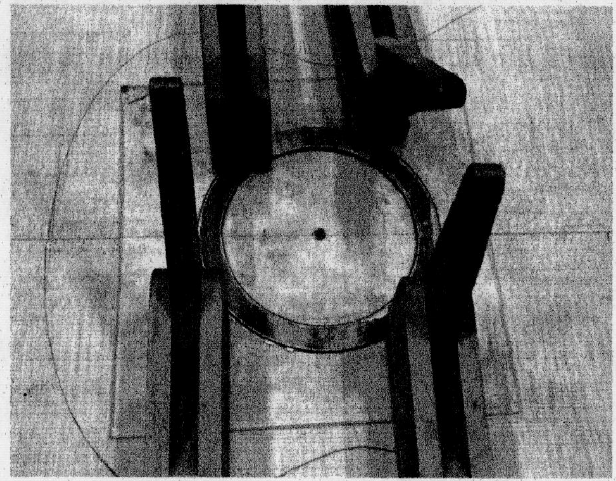

The disc and purfling borders are glued and a clear acrylic caul clamped on top to seat the disc in the channel.

A SOLID TIMBER ROSETTE

The baritone ukulele uses a rosette made from a solid circle of tamarind, an offcut from the timber used for the back and sides. The offcut was thinned to 1.5mm/0.060" and the centre section glued to a plywood substrate. The circle of wood is cut out with a fly-cutter in the drill-press run at low speed. A channel is cut in the soundboard of the appropriate diameter and width, allowing for the veneer or purfling edging.

The finished rosette.

ROPE BINDING ROSETTES

Rope binding is also often used for a matching rosette. The better quality early Hawaiian ukuleles would often have a rosette made of a length of binding edged with a strip of veneer. There might often be a thin line of purfling veneer both on the inside and outside, separated from the centre section by a couple of mm. For a rosette it is best to thin down a couple of the binding strips to 1.5mm/0.060" and cut off the veneer edges. This strip will be around 2.3mm wide if the suggestions in **Chapter 8** on making rope binding were followed. It is hard to bend this strip into the tight circle required, with or without the veneer edging, so the binding strip is

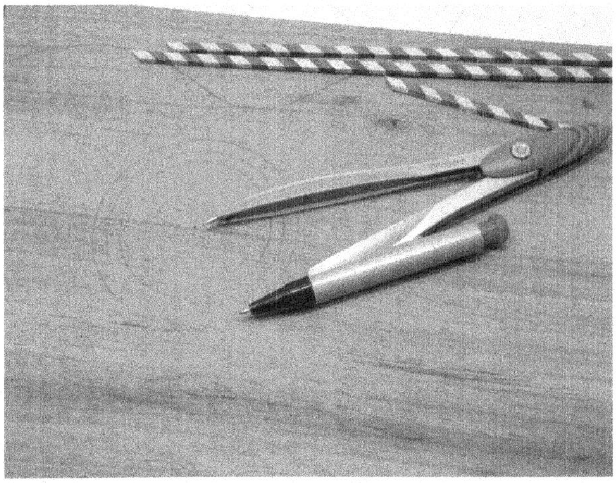

Marking out the soundhole and rosette channel.

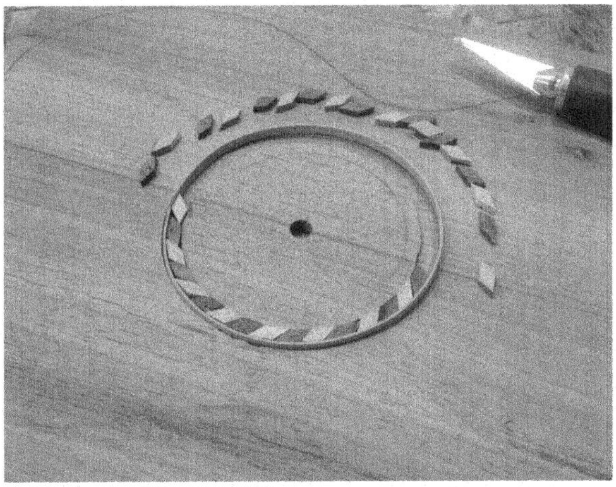

Fitting the segments of the rosette together in the channel with a strip of veneer on the outside. Each segment is slightly trimmed so the fit together neatly in the channel.

Drilling a 3/16" hole for the Stewart-MacDonald circle cutting jig. An auxiliary workboard has a 3/16" hole to match.

Using hot hide glue to individually glue each segment and the veneer edgeing in place, starting from the section closest to the bridge. If the veneer edgings overlap each other accurately the join can be almost invisible.

Below: The channel cut with the Stewart-MacDonald jig.

Below: The finished rosette before levelling.

A heavy scraper is used to level the rosette.

There are many imaginative ways to make a rosette. Above is a mosaic style made by an Australian luthier, Beau Hannam who is now based in Colorado. He glues together a number of small offcuts of exotic timbers and veneers onto a backing sheet. The inlaid rosette is machined from that.

deconstructed into single segment (dark and light) pieces. A narrow strip of veneer 1.5-2mm wide, or a length of 0.5 x 2mm/0.020" x 0.080" wood or fibre purfling is used as new edging strips.

For a simple rope rosette a single circular channel 1.5mm/0.060" deep is cut with a width fractionally over the width of the trapezoidal segments plus the two strips of veneer. For a 2.3mm segment and two 0.5mm purfling veneer strips a channel width of 3.5mm is suggested. Even then the segments, which are still about 4mm/5⁄32" long, will not fit neatly or butt up neatly into the small radius channel. The channel on a soprano has only a 25mm/1" radius and on a concert size around 30mm/1 3⁄16". Trimming a little

Below is a rosette with the channels cut with a CNC router These are a feature of the instruments made by luthier Allen McFarlen of Barron River Guitars in Cairns, Australia. The designs of these minimalist rosettes are programmed into the CNC, cut and then carefully inlaid by hand.

This acrylic base for the Stewart-MacDonald Dremel jig has four 3⁄16" holes to cut four different sized soundholes with a 1.6mm/1⁄16" cutter in the Dremel.

from the acute angle at one end of each segment and a slight tapering on the outside face on the other end will allow the segments to be pushed into place. The two veneer strips need a scarf joint overlap so the join is hidden as there may not be a fretboard to cover this up.

Place the two veneer strips in the channel with an angle cut at one end and slightly over length. The join is usually close to the centreline on the neck side of the soundhole. Start placing the segments from a point opposite the eventual join. Do not use any glue at this time. By the time there is only a couple of segments to be placed, the veneer strips should be pushed firmly onto the outside and inside of the channel and a scalpel blade can be used to accurately cut the other side of the scarf joint on each strip. Finish fitting the segments and adjusting the last couple to look as even as possible, if necessary. Small gaps do seem to disappear visually once the rosette is completed.

Carefully lever out each segment, ensuring that the residual springiness of the veneer strips does not fling a bunch of them across the workspace. Repeat the placing of the segments, this time with glue, using a small flat-head screwdriver or similar to nudge the segments as close together as possible. Hot hide glue is recommended for gluing the segments and the veneer strips as it gap-fills, dries hard and will not show up under the finish later. Titebond or another aliphatic resin can be used, but hot glue is better.

Leave to dry overnight to allow the full evaporation of any moisture and and then finish the thicknessing of the soundboard. As the finished soundboard for a soprano or concert size ukulele is only 1.5mm/0.060" thick, a rosette of the same thickness is going to be a problem. The first step is to reduce the outside surface by .5mm, leaving a 1mm thick rosette, and then only work on the inside surface until the final thickness is achieved.

SOUNDBOARD BRACING

ISLAND SOPRANO

The soundboard of this soprano ukulele has final thicknesses of 1.5mm/0.060". In this case it is made from one piece of Tasmanian blackwood (*Acacia melanoxylon*) a close relative of Hawaiian koa (*Acacia koa*). The soundboards have two transverse braces, above and below the soundhole as well as a small plate (made from a soundboard offcut) underneath the bridge position.

The transverse braces are made from quarter sawn spruce 5mm/3⁄16"wide x 10mm/3⁄8" high with the growth rings parallel to the wider side. This means that when the braces are glued to the soundboard the growth rings will be perpendicular to the soundboard itself.

Start by marking the outline and a centreline on both sides. If a rosette has been inlaid that will usually determine the centreline. Cut out the shape of the soundboard carefully, as the thin veneer of the soundboard plate can be quite fragile and brittle. Mark the positions of the braces and bridge patch on the inside. Make sure to keep the centreline marked as this is very useful when assembling the instrument.

Cut the soundhole with a fly-cutter or a router attachment, and glue the bridge patch to the inside. The soundboard is glued to the transverse braces and the sides in the one procedure so the soundboard can be set aside at this point without the braces glued to it. The building of an Old Island style ukulele is covered in **Chapter 12**.

CHICAGO SOPRANO

The construction of the soundboard for the Chicago style soprano ukulele is the same except that the two soundboard braces and the bridge patch are glued to the soundboard before the assembly of the body.

This can be done with just a couple of spring clamps, while a go-bar deck offers ease of use and flexibility in applying clamping pressure. The bars also allow easy access to clean up any glue squeezeout.

Gluing the braces and the bridge patch on a soprano ukulele.

The braces should be cut slightly over-length, extending just past the marked outside edge. They are straight without any arching sanded into them and should be left rectangular whilst being glued.

Start by gluing the two transverse braces. Apply a thin layer of glue along the bottom of the brace and hold it in place while the clamping pressure is applied. Remove any squeezeout with a strip of heavy card or a plastic drinking straw cut at an angle. The aim is to have as little squeezeout as possible while still using enough glue to fully wet both surfaces. Similarly position and clamp the bridge patch.

Once the glue is dry the last 19mm/¾″ on each end can be carved away so the braces are 3mm/⅛″ high just inside the outline. The ends of the braces will be notched into the linings before the soundboard is glued to the sides. Cut the profile of the braces to a pointed arch, as this saves a little weight without sacrificing much stiffness. Sand the braces to 120 or 180-grit and soften the sharp edges. Lightly sand the bridge patch to take off the sharp edges.

CONCERT

The concert ukulele soundboard is 29cm/11″ long and 19.5cm/7⅝″ wide. Guitar builders often use 20cm/8″ wide boards for the soundboards and backs, and it might be possible to find suitable short lengths for a ukulele from a guitar builder or tonewood supplier. At the same time 10cm/4″ wide

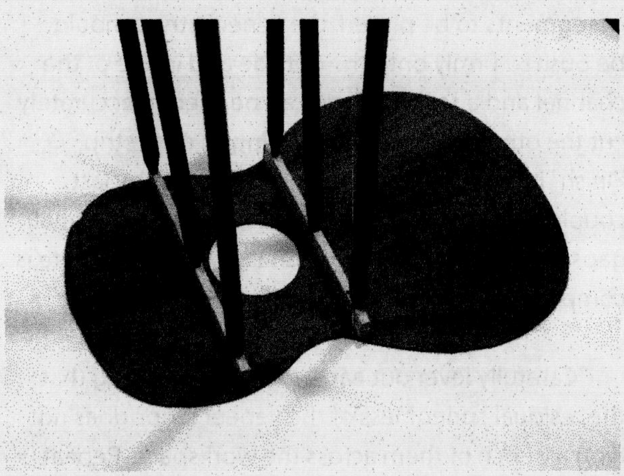

Gluing the two transverse braces on a concert ukulele soundboard.

timber is easier to find, less expensive and can be cut on a 14″ bandsaw. Using narrower timber means that two sequentially cut pieces have to be joined so the grain pattern of the wood is a mirror image, or 'book-matched' on either side of the centre join.

This soundboard is made from mahogany (*Swietenia macrophylla*) and will also have a final thickness of 1.5mm/0.060″. In addition to the two transverse braces, above and below the soundhole, the concert ukulele has two longitudinal braces which fan out from the lower transverse brace towards the tail. If they extended above the soundhole, their theoretical meeting point would be on the body centreline where the neck joins the body. The fan braces sit underneath the ends of the bridge. A small plate 19mm/¾″ wide, again made from an offcut from the soundboard, is glued between the braces underneath the bridge position. Two

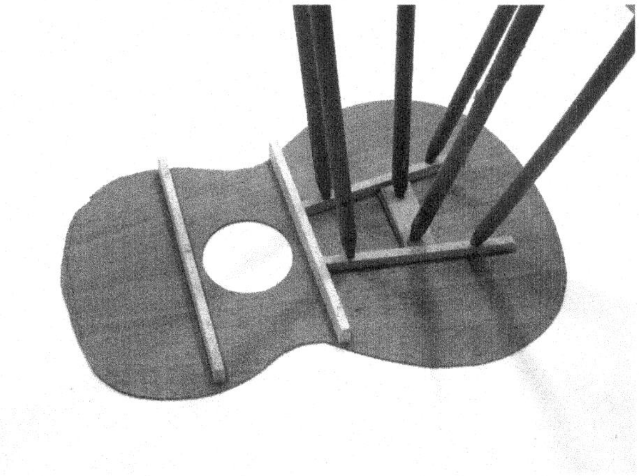

Gluing the bridge patch and the two fan braces on a concert the ukulele.

Carving the concert ukulele braces. The two fan braces are 5mm/3⁄16" wide and 6mm/¼" high.

Adding the two small 5mm/3⁄16" x 5mm/3⁄16" soundhole re-enforcement braces on the concert size.

small lengthways braces are glued between the transverse braces on either side of the soundhole. The soundhole is a weak point in the structure of the soundboard and these two small braces help offset any tendency for soundboard distortion around the soundhole.

The transverse braces are made from the same size material as on the soprano, with the two fan braces the same width but need only be 6mm/¼" high. The two soundhole braces need only be 5mm/3⁄16" square.

TENOR

The tenor soundboard is larger again, being 30.5cm/12" long and 23cm/9" wide. On the first of the tenor instruments the soundboard is made from Californian redwood (*Sequoia sempervirens*) thinned to 2mm/0.080", but it could have been mahogany to match the rest of the body. The main difference in the bracing pattern is the use of three fan braces rather than two. The centre brace is notched to fit over the small plate under the bridge.

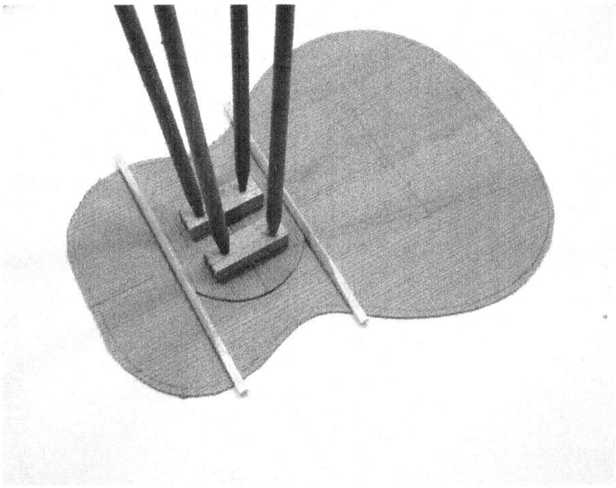

Gluing a soundhole re-enforcement plate between the transverse braces on a tenor ukulele soundboard.

On this ukulele the two longitudinal soundhole braces have been replaced by a thin offcut (1mm/0.040") of the soundboard with the grain running at 90° across the soundboard. The diameter of the disc is a little greater than the outside of the rosette and it is truncated top and bottom to fit between the transverse braces. This re-enforcement should be fitted before the soundhole is cut. Again the purpose of this is to provide extra support around the soundhole. Either this solid support or the two braces can be used on any of the instruments.

The scalloping of the ends of the braces can start a little further in from the ends - 25mm /1"- with the cross-section shaped to a pointed arch.

The finished tenor soundboard. The three fan braces are 5mm/$\frac{3}{16}$" wide and 6mm/$\frac{1}{4}$" high.

BARITONE

The baritone ukulele is the largest of the four instruments and unsurprisingly has the largest soundboard and the deepest body. The soundboard is 35.5cm/14" long and 30.5cm/12" wide across the lower bout. This soundboard is made from Sitka spruce (*Picea sitchensis*) 2mm/0.080" thick. The same basic fan bracing system is employed, but with 5 light fan braces which, if extended, would meet on the body centreline at the neck/body join.

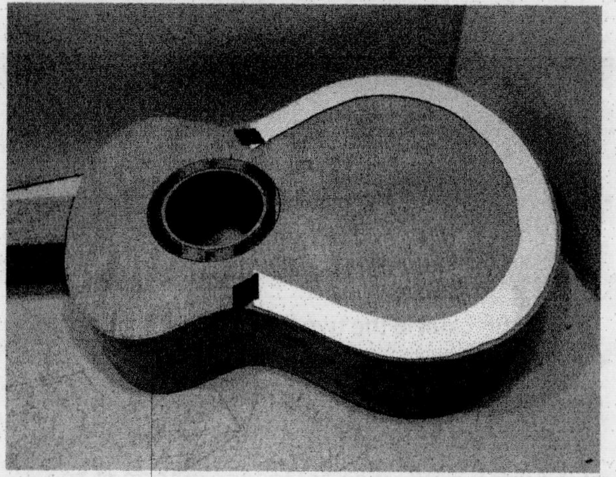

The edging strip of card to support the slight arching of the baritone soundboard.

The baritone ukulele has a slight arching across the lower bout. The upper transverse brace is still flat, the lower transverse brace is slightly curved, so the ends drop away 0.75mm/0.030" from the centre to the edges. A 25mm/1" crescent of 600gsm card is used around the edge of the soundboard to support that curve. 600gsm card is close to 0.75mm/0.030" thick and an equivalent should be available in non-metric countries.

Gluing the transverse braces and the bridge patch in the go-bar deck.

When the glue is dry scallop away the ends of the braces to 3mm/$\frac{1}{8}$" high where they will hit the sides. Again, the cross-section of the braces can also be shaped to a point saving a little weight while not losing stiffness.

Glue the bridge patch in the same way, followed by the fan braces. For the tenor and baritone ukuleles the centre fan brace will have to be notched over the bridge patch. The fan braces are butted up and glued to the lower transverse brace. They are tapered down to 1.5mm/$\frac{1}{16}$" high at each end and the centre section shaped to a point.

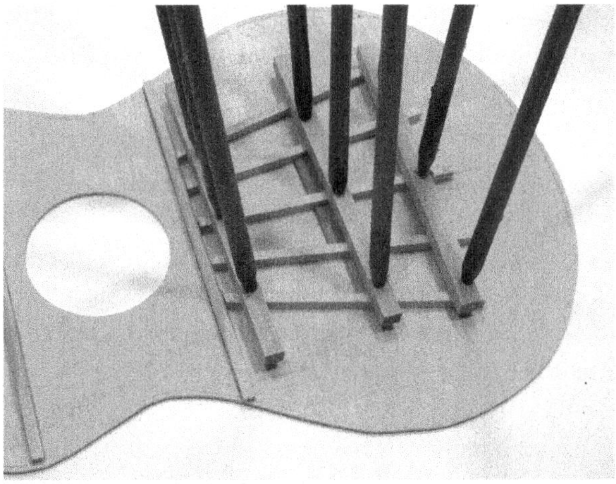

Gluing the five fan braces in the one procedure with scrap off-cuts used to spread the clamping pressure.

If a soundhole re-enforcement patch was not used, two small 5mm/3⁄16" square braces should be fitted between the transverse braces on all ukuleles other than the soprano.

The completed baritone ukulele soundboard bracing. The five fan braces are 5mm/3⁄16" wide and 6mm/¼" high.

Once the bracing is finished, trim the outline of the soundboard to within 1-2mm of the marked outline. If it is an integral neck style of construction the soundboard has to fit precisely into the shape of the ledge, especially where the neck, soundboard and sides meet. The length of the two transverse braces need to be trimmed so they finish the thickness of the sides inside the marked outline. The two transverse braces are an important part of fitting the soundboard to the sides when assembling the ukulele body. The braces should be sanded to 120-grit paper (180-grit for the obsessive) and the soundboard put aside until the body is assembled.

THE BACK

The back of a ukulele is made much in the same way as the soundboard. The back is a thin sheet of wood 1.5-2mm/0.060-0.080" thick made from one or two pieces of timber. It is usually arched, glued to one or more curved braces to allow some movement in changing humidity levels. The body depth of a ukulele tapers from the tail to the neck join and the theoretical profile of the sides can be a complex curve.

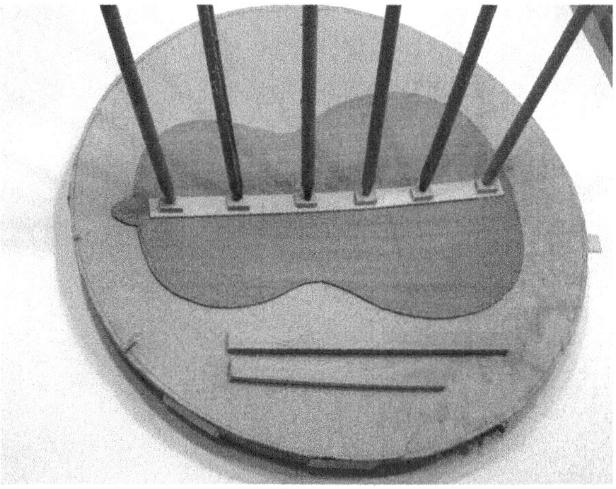

A cross-grain centre re-enforcement strip being glued on a back using a dished workboard which matches the curvature of the braces.

The simplest approach is that used on the early Hawaiian made ukuleles, which used a straight taper from the tailblock to the neck and a single arched brace slightly below the waist. The sides and back linings were probably slightly beveled before the back was glued in one procedure to the sides, linings, blocks and the transverse brace. This is the same methodology 19th century Spanish and Portuguese guitar makers used to attach the backs to their guitars, simplified to the single transverse brace.

The modern approach is to glue the brace or braces to the back and then sand the sides, linings and blocks into a section of a sphere using a concave dish lined with sandpaper. The sides are roughly shaped with a chisel or plane, the linings glued in place and the sanding disc rotated around an axle until the required shape is attained.

The first step is to glue the two haves of the back together (if required) and thin the material down to almost final thickness, which should be 1.5mm/0.060" for a soprano or concert size, and 2mm/0.080" for a tenor or baritone. A two piece back will benefit from re-enforcement to the centre glue join. Guitars use a soundboard off-cut with the growth rings at 90° to the centre seam. Most soundboard material for guitars is supplied longer than is needed and guitar builders will usually have a stash of spruce or cedar off-cuts for this purpose. For a ukulele this strip needs to be 12-15mm/½-⅝" wide and no more than 2mm/0.080" thick. Sand the edges smooth, taking care not to break the strip as the end grain is along the length of the strip and it is quite easy to end up with several shorter strips. The centre strip should be a little longer than the distance between the neck and tail-blocks so it can be trimmed to clear each block before the back is glued in place.

An alternative re-enforcement are a few cross-grain cleats made from off-cuts of the soundboard or back. These are usually cut in a diamond shape 13-18mm/½-¾" in size and can be rub-glued into place after the transverse braces are fitted.

A go-bar deck and a concave sanding dish is best for gluing the back-strip with short off-cut scraps distributing the pressure. A line of masking tape on either side will keep the strip in line as well as collect any glue squeeze-out. Once the glue is dry, round over or bevel the edges with a chisel followed by 120-grit sandpaper.

Mark the centreline and the position of the back braces square to the centreline. The back braces can be made from the same material as the soundboard braces, 5mm/3⁄16" wide x 12mm/½" high spruce for the three smaller ukuleles and 6mm/¼" wide x 15mm/⅝" high for a baritone. These braces start out a little higher than the soundboard braces, but one edge will be shaped to a 12-15' radius curve matching that of the sanding dish, enough to add a 2-3mm/3⁄32-⅛" arch

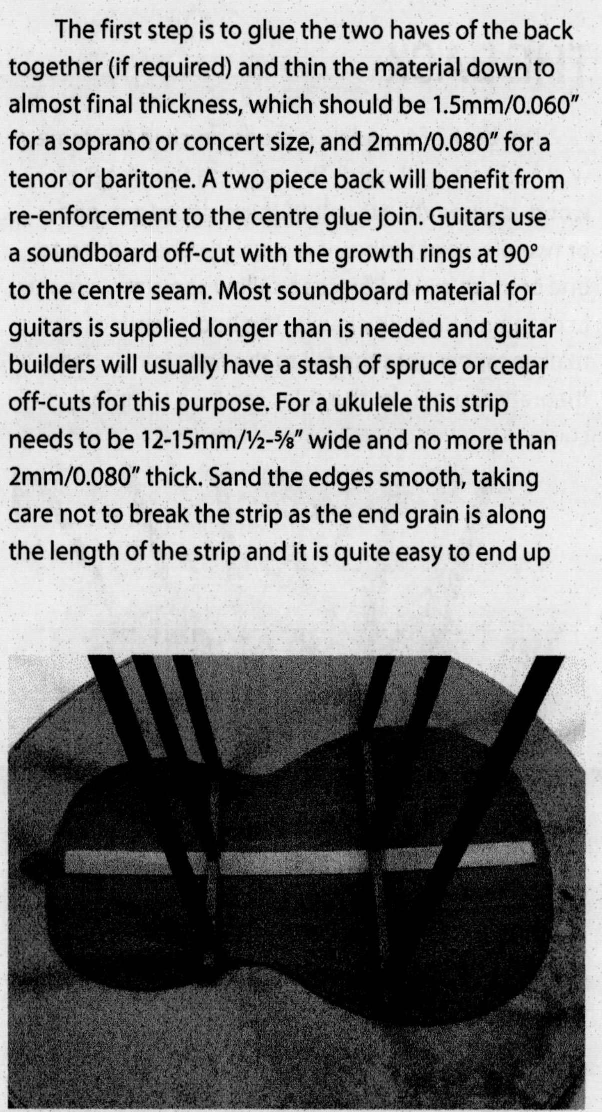

Gluing the two back braces on a concert ukulele using the dished workboard with a matching radius curve as support.

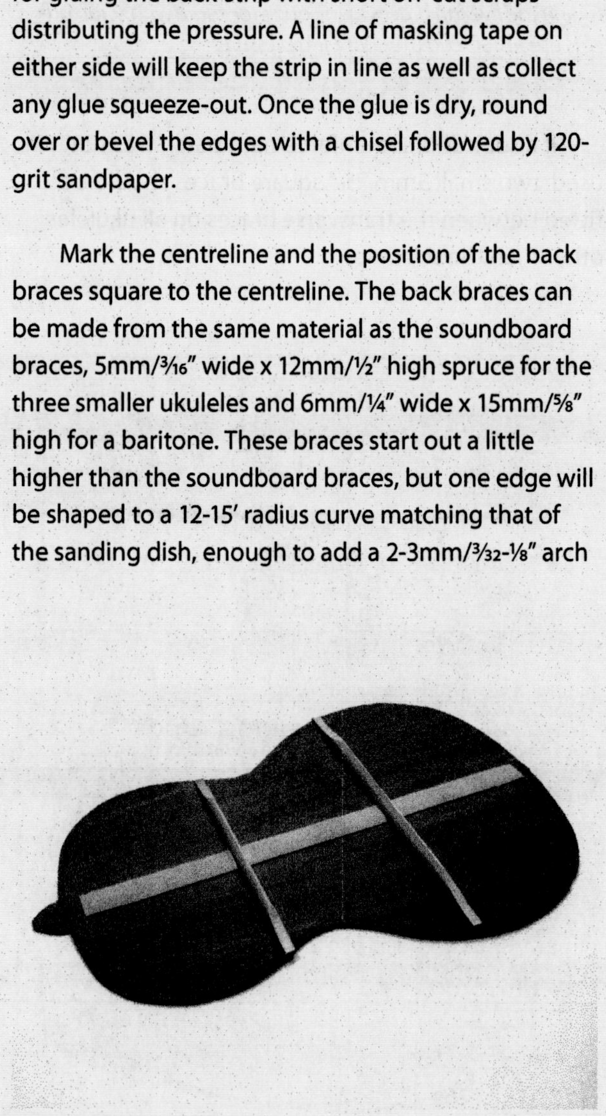

The finished concert ukulele back. The centre strip will be trimmed to neatly fit between the neck and tail blocks.

across the width of the body. The soprano has one brace, the concert and tenor two and the baritone ukulele has three back braces. The shape can be done with a chisel or a plane following a pencil mark and on a disc sander. The sanding dish can be used to refine the curve to match that of the dish.

Mark the width of the braces on the centre strip, cut the notch with a knife or a wide chisel and remove the waste with a smaller 3mm/⅛" chisel. Sand off the pencil line down the middle of the strip as it is easier to do that before the braces are glued. Apply glue and clamp the braces. Once dry, shape the top of the braces to a point with a medium chisel and scallop the last 35mm/1½" of each end of the brace to 3mm/⅛" high where the braces will meet the back linings. Sand smooth with 120-grit sandpaper or 180-grit for a more polished look.

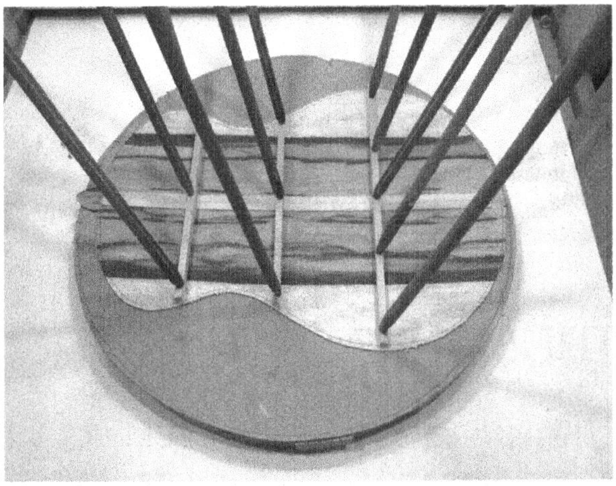

Gluing the three back braces on the baritone ukulele.

Below: The completed baritone back ready for gluing to the sides.

CHAPTER 5
SIDES & LININGS

THE SIDES

There are several ways to bend the sides of a ukulele. All require a combination of heat and moisture to bend the thin slats of timber into the required shape.

Depending on the style of ukulele being constructed, the sides will be between 1.5-2mm/0.060-0.080" thick. The pieces of timber can be brought to the desired thickness with a well sharpened and fettled hand plane and scrapers, but it is much easier to do this with a drum sander of some kind. Almost all guitar builders will have such a machine, as will many co-operative community woodworking groups. For a small charge, and perhaps the cost of a roll of 80-grit sandpaper, it should be possible to get access to such a device. Sand to within 0.25mm/0.010" of the required thickness and remove the scratches with a scraper or an handheld orbital sander. Most timbers will bend quite easily at that thickness, but inevitably there will be some pieces of wood which will simply not cooperate.

The parts list for each style of ukulele gives the length of side required, allowing 25mm/1" extra at each end.

The depth of ukulele bodies tapers from the tail to the neck join. This means that the width of the sides will decrease from the tail to the neck. It is possible to pre-shape the sides to that taper before bending, but it is suggested that this shaping is done after the sides are bent and glued to the neck and tail blocks. Make sure that the edge of each side that will meet the soundboard is straight.

The sides are usually two book-matched pieces of wood, arranged so the grain pattern meets in a mirror image at the tail. It is useful to mark each piece with chalk or a chinagraph pencil so as to be able to ensure the grain pattern will match after the wood has been bent.

THE HOT PIPE

The simplest way, at least in terms of the equipment needed, is using a length of metal pipe heated to around 180°C/350°F. A propane torch is often used, as are oven heating elements or even large halogen light bulbs. Using such heaters elements at mains/line voltage would need careful attention to insulation and earthing/grounding. There are commercially made and electrically heated bending irons available from lutherie suppliers with an oval cross-section.

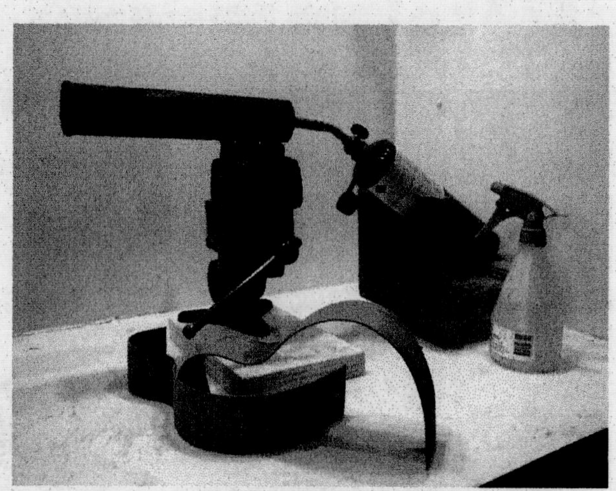

A propane torch, a length of pipe held in a vise and a spray bottle are all that is required to bend the sides of a ukulele.

For a ukulele a 25-30cm/10-12" length of 38mm/1½" pipe is needed with one end mostly closed off. The important consideration is that the radius of the pipe is less than the tightest radius of the chosen body outline. A bracket needs to be made to securely hold the pipe either horizontally or vertically and the propane torch firing into the open end. The one illustrated is a length of brass pipe, with a pop-riveted cap on one end made from a small piece of brass sheet and a simple bracket, also from sheet brass, on the other end. The propane torch gets the pipe to working temperature within a few minutes. The pipe is ready for bending when water sprayed onto the pipe bounces off, rather than sitting there sizzling.

Bending a side over a hot pipe for the first time can be a daunting experience and it does take some practice. If the pipe is not hot enough the wood will not bend and too hot will lead to scorch marks on the wood which can be difficult to sand out. At the right temperature, and this can be different for different timbers, the damp piece of wood will almost magically become plastic and bend into a curve.

The trick is finding the right amount of the side to heat at one time, using a slow but continuous rocking action. It is best to measure where the waist will be, keeping in mind the book-matching of the two sides and bend the waist first.

An electric bending iron. Image courtesy Luthiers Mercantile.

There is a balance to be found between heating only a narrow strip and over-bending it or trying to heat too wide a strip and it not bending at all. At the same time the area to be bent will require spraying with water regularly to help the steam soften the wood. Around the waist it can be better to try a section 25mm/1" at a time, but on the gentler curve of the lower bout it can be possible to bend 50-75mm/2-3" in one pass, overlapping the previously bent section slightly. Even if a heat blanket powered bending jig is used, a hot pipe can be very useful for minor (or even major) adjustments to the shape.

SILICONE HEAT BLANKETS AND THE FOX SIDE BENDER

Bending forms have been around for decades, usually in larger, production oriented factories. They are heated electrically or by steam with pneumatic pressure to bend the sides into shape and not really suited to the one person shop. It was not until the 1970s that an alternative was developed by Charles Fox while a partner in one of the first American guitar building schools, based in Vermont. The Fox Universal Side Bender has become a basic piece of equipment in most guitar building workshops with many variations developed on Fox's original design. The heat source in the 1970s was two or three high wattage incandescent light bulbs, typically 150W. Changes in lighting technology have meant that such bulbs have become scarce, but the ready availability of silicone heat blankets has made the Fox bender even more versatile.

Heat blankets are a silicone rubber mat, usually 1.5mm/1⁄16" thick, with embedded heating elements set for 110v as common in the USA or 220-240v in most of the rest of the world. They heat up to 200°C/400°F within a minute or two and can ignite a piece of wood. Many have an inbuilt thermostat and a heat controller, but they are still dangerous and should not be left unattended.

A simple male/female mould can be used with a heat blanket to bend sides, but there is the disadvantage of the tight curve at the waist not being supported until at least half way through the bending process. Brittle or fragile timbers can easily crack. The

Fox bender's great advantage is supporting the waist curve until it is bedded firmly in the form. A metal bar (in this case a piece of ¼" x 1" aluminium) is held by springs underneath the shaped waist caul. This clamps a wood and heat blanket 'sandwich' together as it is pushed into the waist of the form.

The shop-built Fox style bender illustrated is a smaller version of those used for guitar sides. It will take forms for ukuleles from soprano to baritone size with waist cauls to suit each shape. The size of the springs might need to be adjusted for the different sized forms. The width of each form is 100mm/4" to suit available heat blankets. They are made from two pieces of 15-18mm/⅝-¾" plywood joined by a number of 100mm/4" lengths of 12mm/½'" dowel. These forms could also be made from solid pieces of glue laminated beams that are used in the construction industry. The forms are 2mm smaller than the outline of the ukulele and are notched to sit over the lower framework of the jig so the waist of each form sits directly under the waist caul. The centreline for each shape is 25mm/1" from the bottom of the form to allow some extra length of the bent sides. The waist caul is pressed into position by a veneer press clamp mounted at the top. The bender in the photograph uses a veneer press clamp found in a junk shop and the height of the bender was designed around that particular unit. Similar devices are available from woodworking tool shops. The design of the bender should be based on the size of the bending forms to be used and the length of the veneer press clamp .

The sliding cauls can be no more than a piece of wood with a screw in each end for the springs to hook around. The cauls on this version are slightly fancier with a handle for ease of use.

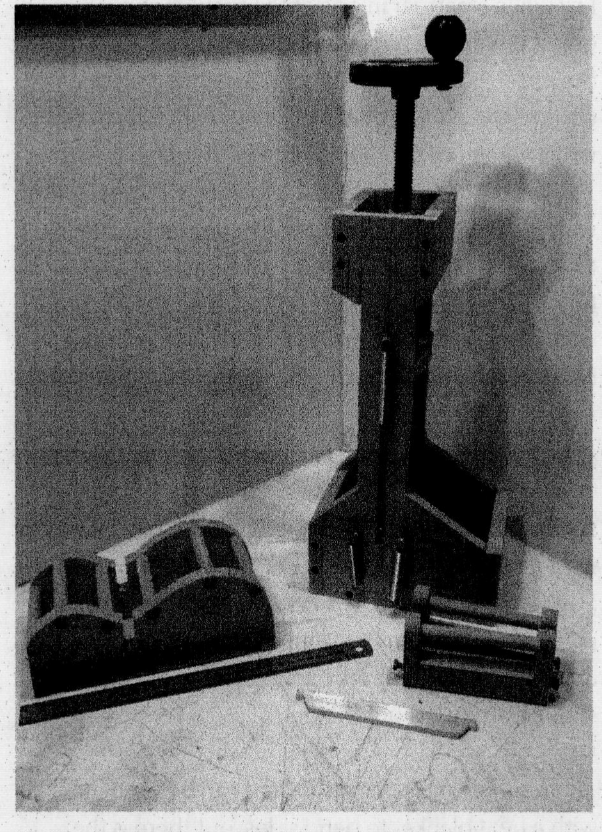

The Fox bender disassembled. The 30cm/12" rulers will give a sense of the size. The base of the jig is 20cm/8" long and the height of the plywood structure is 40cm/16". The slot for the waist support bar is visible in the bending form.

The jig ready for bending. A variety of springs are kept for different sized forms.The slots in the bottom of the form fit over the end plates of the bending jig and locate the waist slot inline with the waist support bar.

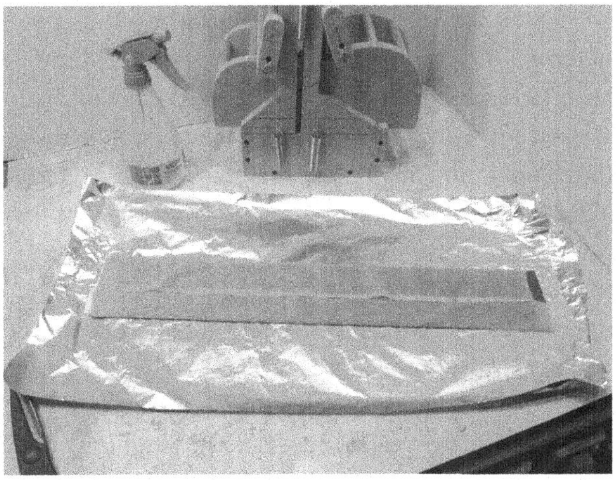

The timber slat wrapped in damp kitchen paper(or kraft paper) ready to be wrapped in aluminium foil.

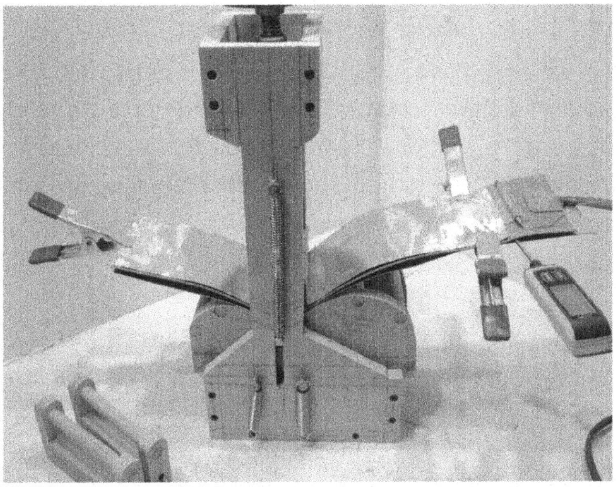

The blanket is turned on, the sandwich is brought up to temperature and the waist caul gradually screwed down to seat the waist caul fully in the form. A digital thermometer monitors the heat.

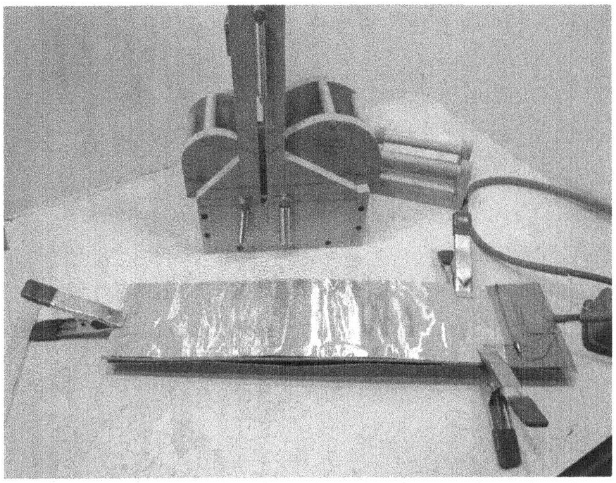

A sandwich is made from the aluminium sheet, the wrapped timber, the heat blanket and the aluminium flashing. A mark can be made a set distance from the front of the sandwich to show the waist position.

The waist caul is fully screwed down and the sliding cauls ready to bend the upper and lower bouts.

The sandwich inserted into the bending jig and the waist caul screwed down so the lower layer of 1mm sheet aluminium is touching the upper and lower bouts of the form.

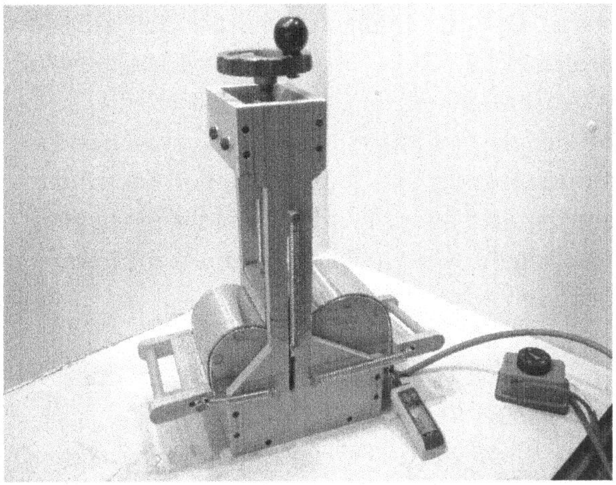

The sliding cauls are pulled down and the upper and lower bouts bent to the form.

BENDING SIDES WITH THE FOX BENDER

Ukulele sides are usually a little thinner than the sides of a guitar: around 1.5mm/0.060" for a soprano or concert model, 1.75mm/0.070" for a tenor and 2mm/0.080" for a baritone. For the ukuleles in this book the lengths of the pieces of wood needed are:
Soprano: 40cm/15.75"
Concert: 49cm/19"
Tenor: 52cm/20.5"
Baritone: 60cm/24"
This allows an extra 2.5cm/1" at each end.

The sides are bent in a sandwich. On the bottom is a piece of 1mm aluminium sheet, 100mm/4" wide and as long as the side to be bent. An alternative is thin shim or spring steel, 0.2mm/0.008" thick, thin enough that it will bend and follow the shape of the form. It does need to be rigid enough to follow the shape across the width of the form. The piece of wood is sprayed with water, and wrapped in a piece of kraft paper or kitchen paper the length of the side and twice the width (so it covers both sides). This is also sprayed lightly to dampen the paper and this in turn is encased in aluminium foil wide enough to be wrapped around the side and overlapped. It should be long enough so the ends can be folded and tucked in to form a sealed package. Care must to taken at this point to remember which is the 'out' side and which end is the neck and tail. This is important for the book-matched appearance of the bent pair of sides.

The heat blanket is placed on top of the wrapped wood and covered by another piece of thin metal sheet. This is 0.3mm/0.011" aluminium roof flashing or .02mm/0.008" steel. The sandwich is held together with a few spring clamps and inserted into the bender, allowing enough to overhang at each end to form a complete side. The waist support bar is fitted and the waist caul screwed down so the sandwich is touching the widest point on the upper and lower bouts of the form.

Turn on the heat blanket set to around 150°C/300°F and wait a couple of minutes. A thermometer is useful to check how hot the sandwich is getting. Steam will escape from a few little gaps and it will smell hot. Wind down the waist caul slowly until it is seated firmly in the form.

Fit the sliding cauls in their springs on either side of the waist caul and pull the sides down onto the form, leaving the cauls clamping the side sandwich at each end. Let it cook for 4-5 minutes and then turn the temperature down to a little over 100°C/212°F and leave for 10 minutes. If the heat blanket has no heat control add a minute or two to the cooking and then turn it off. Turn off and wait until the whole thing cools to room temperature. These temperatures and times are approximate. Different timbers prefer different amounts of moisture and heat and some experimentation may be necessary to minimise 'springback' - the timber wanting to become straight again.

Remember, do not leave the room while the heat blanket is turned on!

Wind the waist caul back up, remove the sandwich and unwrap it. It should be close to the correct shape. There may need to be some adjustment with a hot pipe to refine the curves. A light spray with water and gentle pressure is usually all that is needed. A simple form can be made from MDF and short lengths of dowel to hold the bent side while it dries completely.

LININGS

Except for a small section glimpsed through the soundhole, the linings do not get seen on the finished instrument. They do play an important role in adding rigidity to the structure, as well as providing extra gluing area for the soundboard and back. The idea is that stiffer sides will not absorb the strings' energy as readily and more of that energy becomes sound.

There are two main kinds of linings - solid and kerfed - as well as the separate little triangular blocks of wood - *tentallones* - used in the integral neck style of construction to hold the sides to the soundboard.

Solid lining are strips of timber 8mm/5⁄16" high and 2-2.5mm/0.080-0.100" thick bent to the same shape as the sides. 2.5mm/0.100" is about as thick as can be bent easily. Usually two strips are laminated on the soundboard edge, while one is sufficient for

Cutting tentallones from piece of timber machined to a triangular cross section 7mm x 5mm/9/32 x 3/16″.

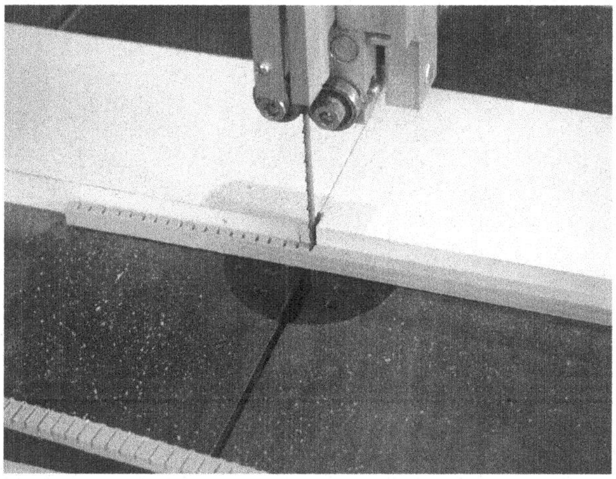

Cutting the kerfing slots in a rectangular strip for a 'reverse kerf' strip. The jig is simply a piece of 16mm melamine covered MDF with a slot cut to clear the bandsaw blade and clamped to the saw table so the blade cannot cut completely through the kerfing strip.

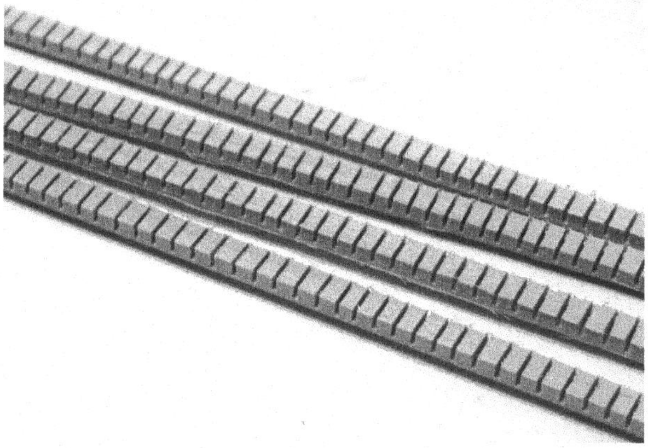

Reverse kerfing strips ready for use.

gluing the back. They can be hand bent on a hot pipe or a bunch of them taped together and bent in a Fox style bender. Off-cuts from the sides themselves are often used. The ukuleles in this book use solid linings of Pacific kauri (*Agathis macrophylla*) a fast growing tropical softwood. Commonly used timbers include mahogany, basswood or Port Orford cedar but almost any light-medium weight timber can be used.

Kerfed linings have the advantage of not needing to be pre-bent. The major lutherie suppliers sell suitable kerfed linings (smaller than standard guitar size linings) or they are easy enough to make with a table or band-saw and a simple jig. A 6 x 8mm/1/4 x 5/16″ strip is planed down to an almost triangular cross section and slots are cut every 5-6mm/ 3/16-1/4″ leaving an uncut strip 0.75mm/1/32″ thick on the wider edge. This is the section which is glued to the sides.

A variant on standard kerfed linings is the 'reverse kerf' where the strips are left rectangular and the uncut section faces inside the instrument. Usually the inside edge is rounded over or bevelled for a neater appearance. At least one company offers kerfed linings where the uncut edge is re-enforced with a flexible veneer which allows tight bends with a reduced chance of breakage.

The linings need to be held in place with a number of small clamps while the glue dries. Wooden clothes pegs have been the traditional choice, often with a small rubber band looped several times around to increase the clamping pressure. A notch can be cut out of one side to fit neatly over triangular kerfing. In recent years the quality of wooden clothes pegs has deteriorated and at the same time small plastic bodied clamps have become cheaper and more available. Either can be used.

THE TAILBLOCK

The tailblock is a piece of spruce, pine or a light hardwood at the tail to which the sides, soundboard and back are glued. They are made 5cm/2″ wide, 13mm/½″ thick and a little longer than the sides are wide to allow trimming. A tailblock made from a single piece of timber can have the grain running with or at right angles to the grain of the sides.

If the grain of the tailblock runs at right angles to the sides, the cross grain of the tailblock helps stop cracks in the sides. This does mean that the soundboard and back are being glued to the endgrain of the tailblock, which is not preferred. (This is usual for violin family instruments, but there is an expectation that soundboard and backs will be taken off for repair at some point in the instrument's life.) Rotating the block so the grain runs parallel to the sides solves the endgrain problem, but an impact can split the block and the sides.

Laminating a three ply block out of spruce both strengthens the block against cracking and avoids most of the endgrain gluing. The outside laminations are 5mm/3⁄16″ thick and have their grain parallel to the sides while a 3mm/⅛″ middle lamination has the grain running vertically. For the tenor and baritone size ukuleles the centre lamination is increased to 5mm/3⁄16″.

Once glued together, start by flattening one end of the block, which will be glued to the soundboard. Mark the 5cm/2″ width of the block at right angles to the flattened surface and machine them flat and square. Trim the height of the block to a little (3mm/⅛″) over the final height, depending on which size ukulele is being built. This will allow for final shaping to follow the curvature of the back and then shape the curve on one face to fit curve of the sides.

Three piece of spruce, 5mm/3⁄16″, 3mm/⅛″ and 5mm/3⁄16″ thick ready to be glued together. The grain runs side to side in the thicker pieces and up and down in the thinner, centre piece.

Below: Two laminated tail blocks.

The template used for cutting out the inside mould form can also be used to trace the convex shape to the laminated block. This can then be shaped on a disk sander or by hand with a plane and sandpaper. Mark a vertical centreline all around. A concave caul of matching size and shape to assist when gluing the sides to the block can be made from a piece of scrap plywood or solid timber. A caul is not necessary when using a solid outside mould.

CHAPTER 6
NECKS

The neck of a ukulele can be made in several different ways. The important thing is that the timber used is dry and stable and not prone to twisting or warping. Nevertheless the builder will usually only find that the piece of wood is not stable and likely to move only after it has been shaped and attached to the body of the instrument. It can be useful to make the neck blank using whatever technique is decided upon, then cut out the profile of the neck and leave that to sit in the workshop environment for a few weeks to allow for any twistng or warping.

The neck can be built integral to the body, with the soundboard, back and the two sides all being glued to the neck itself in the manner of Spanish classical guitar building. Alternatively, the neck can be made separately from the body and attached by a variety of methods. These can include:

- gluing the end of the neck to the body, either directly or using dowels to accurately locate the position;
- using a tapered dovetail joint that physically holds the neck in place (usually glued as well);
- fitting the tapered neck heel into a tapered mortice in the body in the manner of a violin;
- A mechanical attachment using a threaded metal insert and a small bolt.

The last two methods will be used to build the soprano and tenor sized ukuleles respectively. The concert and baritone instruments are built in the Spanish style.

If the neck is built separately, consideration has to be given to attaching it to the body so the centreline of the neck lines up with the centre of the body. In addition the top surface of the neck has to be in the same plane as the soundboard, both lengthways and across. Building the neck separately certainly has advantages in a factory production environment where jigs and power tools can ensure consistent mating of the body and neck. For someone building a few ukuleles an integral neck can make more sense and be easier to get right.

The integral neck as well as the tapered mortise and bolt-on methodologies will be described and can be used for any size ukulele, although fitting a bolt in through a soprano ukulele's soundhole could be trickier than is worthwhile. The tapered dovetail is a very strong and robust joint and has been used by the C.F.Martin company for their ukuleles for over a century but is a stronger and more complex joint than might be necessary.

The string tension on a ukulele is relatively light and there is no real need for re-enforcement to off-set the pull of the strings as would be required for a steel string guitar. A carbon-fiber bar or tube could be set into the shaft of the neck if the timber seemed particularly light and flexible, but usually the neck timber and the attached fingerboard provide enough strength to cope with the string tension.

With the exception of the Old Island style of soprano (see **Chapter 12** for details), all the ukuleles built for this book have common fretboard widths of 35mm/1⅜" at the nut and 45mm/1¾" at the 12th fret so any timber or glued up block used to make a neck needs to be a minimum of 45mm/1¾" wide.

NECK CONSTRUCTION

The width of the materials required for the neck is determined by the design of the head. Most commercial ukuleles use a design at least 6cm/2⅜" wide. A minimum width of 6.5cm/2½" is suggested for whichever of the following approaches is used.

1. THE SOLID BLOCK

The simplest way to make a neck is to cut it out of a solid block of timber 6.5-7.5cm/2½-3" square and a little longer than is needed for the neck. The block should be quarter-sawn or as close to it as possible, especially along the top surface of the neck. It is the most wasteful and expensive way to make a neck as most of the wood it cut away. The remnants are too small to do much with other than make things like the tail-block.

Above: A neck cut from a 3.5cm/1½" block of solid wood with an extra piece ready to be glued onto the heel to make up the required depth of the heel.
Below: The extra piece glued in place.

Three laminates of Australian red cedar ready for gluing into a block.

Above: The laminated block glued and clamped.

Below: The laminated block ready to be used. The holes for the locating dowels can be seen clearly.

2. THE BUILT UP HEEL

A more economical approach is to use a shallower block, 3.5cm/1½" deep, that allows the angled head to be cut in one piece. An offcut is laminated to the other end to make sufficient depth for the heel. The style of construction was often found on early Hawaiian made ukuleles. An almost un-noticeable heel lamination can be made if the initial board is at least 5cm/2" longer than the overall neck length. The extra length can be cut off and glued on to form the heel extension. The side slots can be cut and the neck shaped as if it were being cut from a solid block.

3. VERTICAL LAMINATIONS

A solid block can be made by laminating two, three or four thin pieces of wood to make up the required width of the neck. This can be useful if there is attractive but non-quartersawn timber available. The endgrain should be arranged so that any tendency to warp will be off-set by the neighbouring lamination. A contrasting timber can be used for a centre laminate. The thickness for each laminate should be selected so there is no join along the outsides of the neck shaft.

The boards to be laminated should be a little oversized, slightly wider than the neck heel is deep and slightly longer. They should be freshly machined (either by a planer or drum sander) and as straight as possible. Clamp them together squarely and drill two 6mm/¼" holes at opposite corners. Two pieces of 6mm/¼" dowel inserted into the holes will keep the laminates aligned under clamping pressure. The dowels should be in the waste sections on top of the head and behind the heel. Use chalk to mark the narrow edges so that the boards can be glued in the same sequence.

Place one board on the bench with the dowels inserted. Smear glue on each board and slide them over the dowels. Apply clamps, clean the glue squeeze-out and leave overnight to dry. Clean up what will be the top surface of the neck, making sure it is square to the sides of the block. The rest of the process is the same as for a solid block of wood.

4. A BUILT UP NECK.

The starting point is a cleanly dressed and preferably quarter sawn board at least 6.5cm/2½" wide and at least 18mm/¾" thick. It has to be long enough to be able to have the head cut from it and reglued at an angle with a scarf joint, as well as enough extra length to allow the stacked lamination of the heel from two or three short pieces 6cm/2⅜" long.

Minimum lengths are:
Soprano - 42cm/16½"
Concert - 45cm/18"
Tenor - 50cm/20"
Baritone - 55cm/22"

Draw a centreline along the length of what will be the top surface. Mark a line across the width and down the sides 12cm/4¾" from one end. On one side of the board draw a line at a 14° angle from that mark back towards the end of the board. Using a hand or bandsaw cut off the small trapezoidal piece which will become the angled head. Cut on the side of the pencil line to leave the full length of the shorter offcut. Clamp the longer remaining piece to the bench with the short offcut on top so the angled faces line up. Using a small plane and a half-sheet sanding block clean up the sawn surfaces. The angled face on the offcut block is especially important as this will be glued to the bottom of the longer piece and has to be perfectly flat in both directions. Doing this while the smaller piece is clamped to the larger piece makes getting the perfectly flat gluing surface on the smaller piece a little easier to achieve.

Making the saw cut for the spliced headstock.

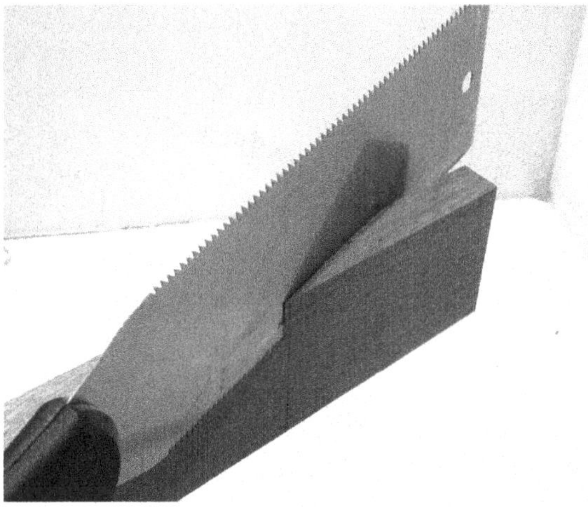

Above: The head offcut is clamped to the remaining neck shaft and the saw cuts planed and sanded until smooth and square.

Below: The spliced head is glued to the neck shaft with acrylic cauls and clamps to stop the pieces sliding around.

The stacked heel glued and clamped.

This can be done on a disc sander, but care must be taken not to sand any convexity into the gluing surface.

Clamp the longer piece on one side to the workbench or the auxiliary workboard with two clamps, leaving enough room at the angled end for the smaller piece to be glued to the bottom surface A piece of thin plastic underneath will stop the neck being glued to the bench from any glue squeeze-out. Apply glue and clamp the short piece to the bottom surface of the neck. Two small (6.5cm/2½"x 6.5cm/2½") pieces of 3mm/⅛" acrylic can be used as clamping cauls on either side with G-clamps holding it together. Another clamp can be used at the end of the short piece to stop it sliding forward, with another holding the narrow edge firmly to the work surface. This is a procedure where it can be useful to try a couple of times without glue to work out the location of the clamps so they do not interfere with each other.

Once the glue has dried clean up the upper face of the head with the plane and sanding block, ensuring that the angle of the head is square to the top surface of the neck. The neck shaft itself is half the head with the scarf-jointed section the end of the neck. The head should be around 12cm/4¾" long, which will accommodate most ukulele head shapes.

Mark the point where the head starts with a pencil and another 3mm/⅛" away from the head which will be the width of the nut. For a soprano or concert size draw another line at the 12th fret position and another 15mm/⅝" beyond that which will be the end of the neck block for a Spanish heel neck. For a tenor and baritone size ukulele the neck block should be 25mm/1" deep. The baritone ukulele is also likely to have 14 frets to the body join rather than 12, so this extra length has to be allowed for. Cut the remainder off, leaving an extra 5-6mm/¼" as insurance.

NOTE*: If a bolt-on neck with an extension to support the fretboard is used (see below) the extra length must be allowed for.*

From the off-cut remainder of the board cut enough 6cm/2⅜" lengths to glue together to make the heel. The body of a soprano ukulele is around 5cm/2" deep at the neck join while a baritone is close to 7cm/2¾" deep, so two or three blocks will be necessary. The final depth of the heel needs to be a little more than the body depth to allow for the tapering of the body. This means that the inside face of the heel will be a mm or so deeper than where the slots for the sides are cut.

Cut and number the pieces sequentially from the off-cut length. This ensures that when the blocks are glued to the main shaft of the neck the grain pattern of the laminated blocks should match quite closely and the laminations be almost un-noticeable. Take care to keep the heel laminations square to the neck surface.

The same acrylic clamping cauls used for gluing the scarf jointed head can be used to keep the heel stack aligned while the glue dries.

CUTTING THE NECK PROFILE

The first step is to make sure the top surface of the neck, to which the fretboard will be glued, is perfectly flat. A half-sheet sanding board is useful for this, checking often with 15cm/6" and 30cm/12" steel rulers for any concavity, convexity or twisting of the surface. The neck profile can then be marked on the side of the neck, whether it is a solid block of timber or a glued-up construction.

The neck should be 13mm/½" deep under the nut and 18mm/¾" deep where the heel begins, which should be between the 8th and 9th fret positions (10th and 11th for a 14 fret tenor or baritone). The bottom of the heel should be no more than 13mm/½" long where it meets the back. Draw a smooth curve from the front of the heel to the 18mm/¾" point, a straight line from there to the 13mm/½" point under the nut and blend that into the tapering head thickness.

Cut out the profile of the neck with a bandsaw leaving a little extra thickness at the head and the heel.

For the violin style tapered mortise neck attachment the neck should be left 6mm/¼" longer to allow for the tapered heel to be glued into the neck block.

THE HEAD OVERLAY

The head thickness tapers from 11mm/7⁄16" thick at a point 30mm/1¼" from the nut to 10mm/⅜" at the end. This will allow most rear-mounted ukulele tuners to be used. If the neck is cut from a solid block the upper face of the head can simply be planed and sanded smooth, but a scarf-jointed head will need a veneer on the upper face to cover the join. A dark timber matching the fretboard, such as rosewood or ebony, is common and lutherie suppliers offer a range of exotic choices. A koa fretboard is also common on koa bodied ukuleles and a fancy piece of koa on the head will match that.

Because the head of a ukulele is thinner than that of a guitar the overlay veneer looks more in proportion if it is around 1mm/0.040" thick, rather than 2mm/0.080" as is common on larger instruments such as guitars. The nut end of the overlay should be cut square and beveled to a 14° angle so it is perpendicular to the neck surface and acts as support for the back of the nut. This can be done with a sanding board or with a disc sander. It can be useful to keep the triangular piece cut from a solid neck blank to use as a guide when using a disc sander.

A Spanish-style neck cut from a solid block. The slots for the sides were cut first by hand.

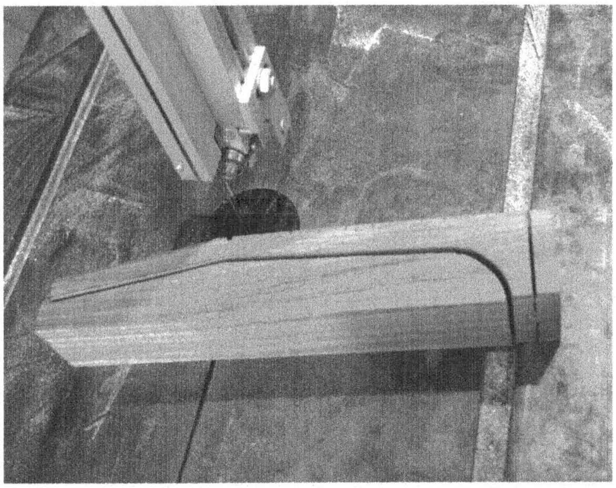

Positioning the head veneer overlay with a machinist's square, an acrylic caul and two spring clamps. The holes for the locating pins have been drilled outside the head shape.

Above: Another way to position the head overlay with the fretboard pinned in position and a bone nut blank used to align and position the overlay.

Below: The veneer overlay pinned, glued and clamped. A piece of 3mm/⅛" acrylic is used the even the clamping pressure.

Clamp a small machinist's square on the line marking the back of the nut and butt the head overlay to that. Hold both in place with spring clamps. Drill two 1⁄16" holes through the veneer - outside the planned outline of the head - and tap in two 1⁄16" pins or nails. A piece of 3-5mm/⅛-3⁄16" acrylic or thin plywood slightly smaller than the veneer will act as a clamping caul to even out the clamping pressure. Drill two larger holes (5mm/3⁄16") in the caul that will clear the heads of the small nails. Apply glue to the underside of the veneer, locate it with the pins, and clamp in place with the caul. Leave overnight for the glue to fully dry.

SHAPING THE HEAD

On the back face of the head mark out the required shape and cut out the head shape. Note that the flare from the nut width to the wider part of the head will be different on the back of the head due to the angle of the head. Cut a couple of mm outside the line, the excess allowing for a little tearout from the bandsaw blade on what will be the upper face.

Finish the tapering thickness of the head, from 10mm/⅜" at the end, to 11mm/7⁄16" at a line 30mm/1 3⁄16" from the nut. This can be done in several ways with chisels, a drill press mounted drum sander or a spindle sander with a fence, or with a Wagner Safe-T-Planer. The original Wagner devices are no longer available, but Stewart-MacDonald sells a very similar device. A 1mm/0.040" thick shim is tack-glued to the overlay on the end of the front of the head to allow the taper to be machined.

Finish the shaping of the head outline with a chisel and a sanding block to the drawn lines and mark the positions of the tuner holes. Drill holes for the posts holding the back of the head to the drill press table. This ensures the holes are vertical to the back face where the tuners will be mounted. The size of the holes will depend on the type of tuner chosen. **Chapter 15** covers the various kinds of tuners.

A 1mm/0.040" spacer lightly glued to the end of the head to allow the Saf-T-Planer to machine a tapered head.

The Saf-T-Planer held in a collet chuck in the drill press/milling machine.

COMPLETING THE NECKS

As the procedures are different for a Spanish heel neck, a violin mortice neck and a bolt-on neck, information on carving and fitting the heels, as well as the final shaping of the neck shaft is contained in **Chapters 9-13**, each chapter dedicated to assembling the various styles of ukulele as well as carving the necks.

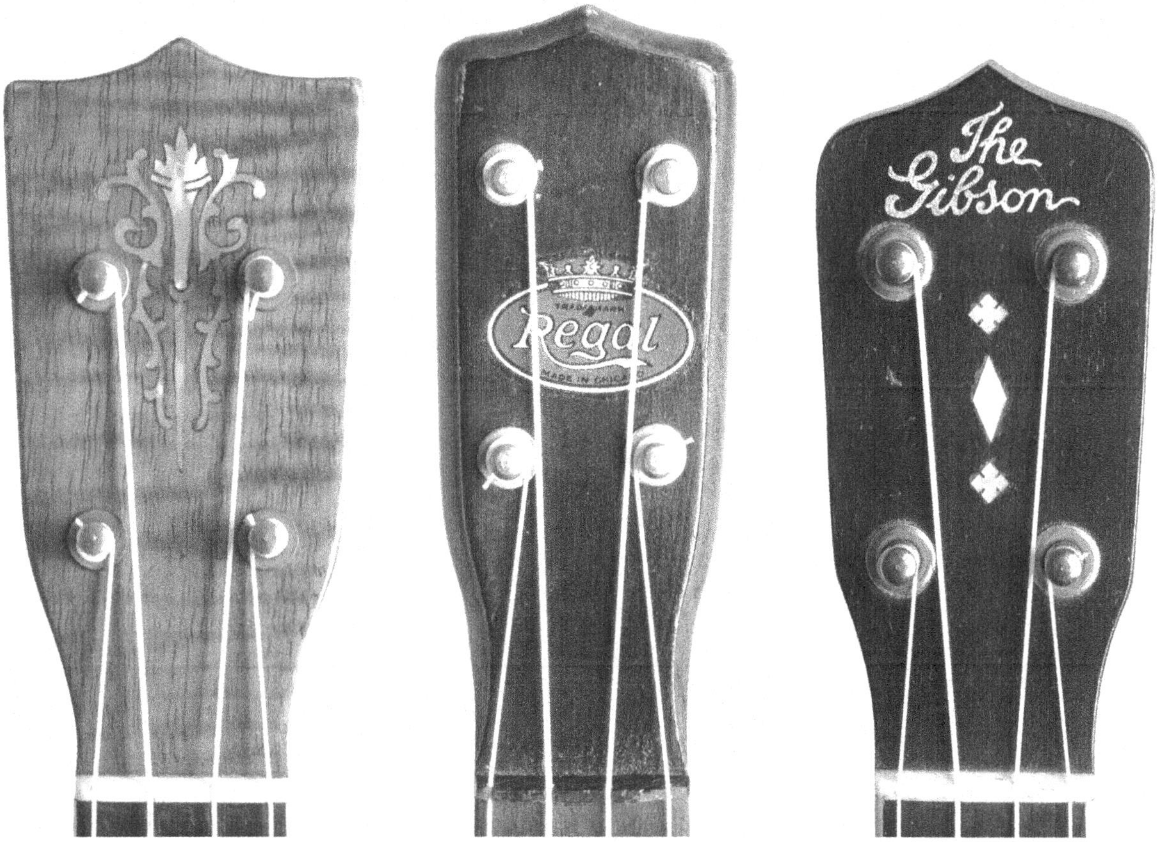

A selection of ukulele heads from the golden era of the 1920s: a 1924 Martin, a 1930 Regal and a 1928 Gibson. The Regal appears to have the edges of the head rounded over with a coving bit on a table router. Images courtesy Retrofret.

CHAPTER 7
THE FRETBOARD

The fretboard is a piece of hardwood, often ebony or one of the rosewoods, with metal frets inserted in slots cut at 90° to the centreline. The slots are precisely positioned by mathematical calculations. Other than for the Old Island style of ukulele described in **Chapter 12**, all the ukuleles use fretboards 35mm/1⅜″ wide at the nut and 45mm/1¾″ at the 12th fret.

The four different size ukuleles all have differing open string or scale lengths. This is the distance between the nut and the bridge saddle.

- Soprano 33-35.5cm/13-14″
- Concert 38cm/15″
- Tenor 43cm/17″
- Baritone 51cm/20″

These are average measurements and can vary from instrument to instrument by up to 12mm/½″. The exact string length is unimportant, the critical thing is the placement of the frets along the fingerboard in relation to that distance.

For several centuries the position of the frets was determined by the simple process of dividing the string length by 18 and repeating that for the number of frets to be used. This can be done graphically once the result of the first division is known. A line is drawn of the required string length and that number is divided by 18. That will be the distance from the nut to the first fret, musically one semitone. A perpendicular line of that distance is drawn at one end and a hypotenuse drawn to form a flattened triangle. A compass is used draw a quarter circle using the perpendicular line as the radius. Another vertical line is drawn to the hypotenuse and another quarter circle will give the distance to the second fret. This is repeated for the number frets to be used. On smaller ukuleles this might only be 12 frets, with the 12th fret located at the neck/body join. On larger models the fretboard extends over the body with up to 19 frets.

This technique was used for many years, even though there are inherent limitations, such as allowing for the thickness of the drawn lines. A better way to do this is by doing multiple long divisions

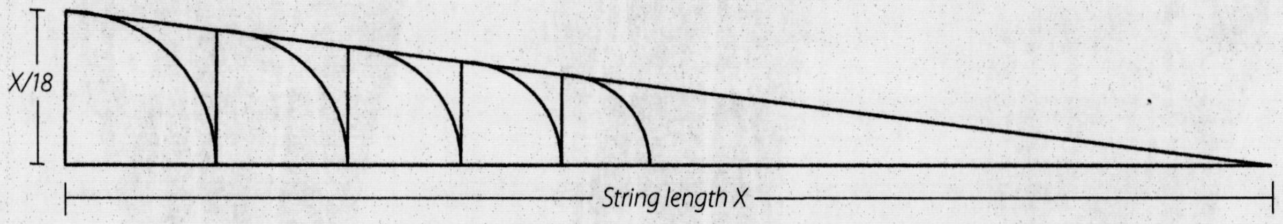

A not-to-scale diagram of a mechanical method of laying out fret positions using the Rule of 18. The distance between the left end and the first arc would be the distance from the nut to the first fret. The second arc would then be the distance from the first to the second fret and so on.

and accurately marking the fret positions on a strip of metal to use as a template. A few minutes with an electronic calculator or setting up an electronic spreadsheet to successively divide by 18 can produce accurate calculated fret positions for any desired scale length.

The Rule of 18 has fallen out of use over the past century in favour of the more mathematically accurate divisor of 17.817 - derived from the 12th root of 2. This puts the 12th fret at the precise centre of the scale length. While mathematically precise this does not work as well musically, as the action of pushing the string down to the frets stretches the string slightly and the note is sharpened. To compensate for this the theoretical scale length is increased by around 2mm/5/64" and the bridge saddle placed that much further down the body.

Dividing by 18 rather than 17.817 means that the fret intervals are slightly smaller, and this builds in the necessary compensation. It does work better for nylon strings rather than steel strings and so is a suitable way of calculating the fret positions on a ukulele. Calculations of fret positions by both methods are printed in the **Appendix**.

Marking fret positions with a steel ruler and a brad-awl.

Scoring a line across for each fret with an X-Acto knife and a machinist's square.

Planing a fretboard blank to thickness. A 3mm/1/8" thick strip at the top end holds the blank on a simple bench hook fixture.

Using a fretting saw with an adjustable depth stop (attached to the opposite side of the blade) and the machinists' square to cut the fret slots.

Fretwire used on ukuleles is usually narrower than that used on guitars, with most suppliers offering suitable fretwire 1.25-1.5mm/0.050-0.060" wide. For many years the only fretwire available was made from a copper alloy known as "nickel-silver" even though it contained no silver and was mostly copper with around 20% zinc and 18% nickel. The percentage of nickel determines the hardness of the wire. 18% is fairly standard, but there is a softer 12% nickel wire.

Restrictions in Europe on the use of nickel where it can come in contact with the skin has led to the use of nickel-free copper alloys such as used in Evo Gold fretwire. As the name suggests it is gold in colour and harder than nickel/silver wire. At the top of the hardness scale is stainless steel, but it is more difficult to work with and harder on tools. For most ukuleles nickel-silver wire is more than suitable.

There is an industry-standard width for fret slots of 0.023" (0.55mm). Lutherie supply houses offer both hand and circular saw blades to cut slots of that size. There are a variety of jigs and templates available to assist with accurately positioning fret slots. Most of the suppliers also offer pre-slotted fretboards. Jigs and templates are useful for cutting fretboards but not absolutely necessary. All that is required is a hand saw with a .023" kerf, a small machinist's square, a 30cm/12" steel ruler and a knife or brad-awl to mark the slot positions.

Fretboards are usually made from a dense hardwood, with ebony and rosewood most commonly used. Suggested thickness for a ukulele fingerboard is 3-4mm/⅛-5⁄32", with the smaller models thinner and the larger tenor and baritone ukuleles using slightly thicker pieces of wood. The slots need to be 2mm/3⁄32" deep to allow enough depth for the fret tang. A depth stop on the saw is useful to avoid cutting right through the fretboard. If a thickness sander is available the board can be left at 5mm/3⁄16" or so thick while the slots are cut and then brought down to final thickness, keeping the slots 2mm/3⁄32" deep.

1mm holes are drilled through the first or second and 10th fret slots and into the neck for 1mm steel nails to hold the fretboard in place when it is glued to the neck.

Mother-of-Pearl dots are glued as fret markers at the 5th, 7th and 12th frets, though there are many other ways to mark the fret positions.

Below: Fret markers inset into the side of the fretboard. These are slices of ivoroid piano keys 1mm/0.040" thick.

The early Hawaiian instruments and many of the cheaper Chicago-built ukuleles simply had the frets set directly into the top of the neck with no separate fingerboard, but almost all modern instruments use a separate fingerboard.

Plane one edge of the board straight to ensure that the fret slots are all parallel. Use a couple of spring clamps to hold the ruler to the board and use a knife or brad-awl to mark the nut and as many fret positions as are needed. A metric ruler is suggested as an accuracy of 0.1mm can be achieved with a little care and good lighting. Mark the fret positions as cumulative distances from the nut, as trying to mark the individual distances between the frets will inevitably lead to inaccuracies. Remove the ruler and mark lines across the width of the board using the square and the knife. Use the square to guide the saw to make the cuts. The knife cuts are a good visual reference to keep everything square during the slot cutting.

Above: Tapping the frets into place with a hammer. The slots are lubricated with a bead of hot hide glue although any wood glue can be used.

Below: Pressing the frets into place with a dedicated tool in a drill press. A brass insert in the bottom of the tool is available in various common fretboard radii.

Mark a centreline on the board a consistent distance from the planed edge to maintain a 90° angle to the fret slots. If the fretboard blank was originally a tapered shape, the penciled centreline may have to be shifted a little to allow for the final outline to fit into the taper.

Once the slots are cut and the board reduced to final thickness (if required) the fretboard can be tapered to final size: 35mm/1⅜" wide at the nut and 45mm/1¾" at the 12th fret. Saw right through the board at the nut slot and trim the other end.

Position markers can be inlaid on the face of the fretboard, usually at the 3rd, 5th, 7th, 10th and 12th frets or some combination of those. The 5th, 7th and 12th fret positions are most common. Plastic or pearl dots of various sizes are available from suppliers and can be superglued into shallow holes usually drilled along the centreline of the fretboard. The thinness of a ukulele fretboard makes it harder to inlay markers along the side of the fretboard, but it can be done with care. 1⁄16" plastic rod is the usual material, but larger markers can be used along the edge of the board which are more visible to the player.

At this point the fretboard can be test-fitted to the neck and body. Hold it in position with spring clamps and make sure everything lines up correctly. 1mm brad point nails are used to locate the board when it is eventually glued to the neck and body. Drill 1mm holes through the 2nd and 10th fret slots into the neck, making sure the drill bit does not go all the way through the neck. The exact size of the nails or pins does not matter, as long as they are smaller than the fret width and the holes will not be seen after the frets are installed.

Before installing the frets the board should be sanded to at least 400-grit as that cannot be done effectively after the frets are in place. Use a straight edge to keep the board flat along the line of the strings. Ukulele fretboards are traditionally flat across their width but a hint of transverse convexity (less than .5mm/.020" drop from centre to edges) can help with the feel of the instrument. It can also offset the ongoing slight shrinkage and cupping of the fretboard over time. Clean out the fret slots and check for a consistent 2mm/3⁄32" depth. A small triangular file can be used to put a slight bevel on the edges of the slots. This can help locate the frets in the slots and assist in preventing chipping if the fret has to be removed.

A solid flat surface is needed under the fretboard to hammer the frets into position. A bead of wood glue along the slot is useful to lubricate the fret as it goes in. Start by tapping in the fret on one end of the slot and work across the width of the board. It should only take a few light taps to seat the fret in the slot and a few more to get the crown of the fret sitting flush with the board. Care must be taken to avoid the hammer face marking the surface of the fretboard. A hardwood caul in a vice can be useful in fully seating the frets, or there are devices which can be mounted in a drill press to push them into place.

After each fret is installed, trim the excess length and remove any glue with warm water and a paper towel. Remember not to instal frets into the slots with the holes drilled for the locating pins. Once the glue has dried file the fret ends flush with the edges of the fretboard with a large medium cut file, and bevel the ends of the frets at a 35-40° down to the fretboard edge.

The fretboard is now ready for gluing to the neck and body. The two extra frets will be installed after gluing.

CHAPTER 8
BINDINGS & PURFLINGS

Binding around the edges of the soundboard and back is not entirely necessary, but it can be visually effective and does prevent impact damage to the edges of the thin plates. Plastic binding, whether modern ABS or the more old-fashioned celluloid, is simple to install. They can be bent into shape as they are being glued with an acetone-based solvent glue. The glue is applied in sections 10-15cm/4-6"long and the binding held in place with masking tape overnight while the solvent evaporates.

Wooden binding can match or compliment the body timbers, but does need to be bent accurately to the body contours before being glued into place. Coloured purflings (thin strips of veneer) or even narrow pieces of pearl or abalone shell can be used inside the binding for added effect. Black and white (BW) purflings are most commonly used but there are a lot of other possibilities. Variously coloured veneers are available for inventive purfling ideas.

If both soundboard and back binding is fitted, it is usual to visually tie them together with a strip which covers the join of the sides at the tail that matches the timber or plastic binding. This strip can either be straight or tapered. On the baritone ukulele shown below the strip is an offcut of one of the tamarind sides and tapers from 11mm /13⁄32" to 8mm/5⁄16" in width along its 80mm/3⅛" length. The binding is also an offcut from the sides. Black fiber purfling is glued to binding strips on the inside and the bottom edges. The strip on the bottom edge was glued to the binding strip before bending. Aliphatic glue was used and the fiber strip held with masking tape. The glue will soften when the binding is bent and there is a danger that the fiber strip will buckle. A clothes iron can be used to flatten any buckling.

The tail strip is glued in place first and the fiber purfling on the binding strip cut away to fit over the tail strip. The binding strips are cut with a scarf joint to minimise the visual overlap.

The binding in this tenor ukulele is tortoisehell celluloid with a strip of black/white purfling. A matching rosette uses two of the binding strips glued together.

The binding and tail graft on the tamarind baritone ukulele. The bindings are sapwood offcuts from the sides with a 0.5mm/0.020" black fiber strip on the inside and bottom edge. The tail graft is a side offcut edged with the black fiber.

ROPE BINDING

Rope binding was commonly found on many early Hawaiian made ukuleles as soundboard edging as well as for the rosette. This style of binding was also used by Hermann Weissenborn on his better quality guitars as well as the eccentrically wonderful guitars and mandolins by Chris Knutsen. You might call it a *Koa Aesthetic* that was all part of the great popularity of Hawaiian music in the 1920s, especially on the West Coast of the USA.

It fell out of fashion for many years, but with the current interest in ukuleles and Weissenborn style steel guitars, rope binding has made a small comeback. The binding is made of small, angled pieces of wood in alternating colours, usually with a strip of veneer purfling in the inside that matches one of the colours used. When the binding is rounded over after being glued on to the instrument it takes on a rope-like appearance.

This style of binding is not hard to make, but requires repeated processes of gluing, slicing and sanding to end up with strips of binding 2-3mm/.080 - .120" square. A drum sander or at least a sanding drum and fence mounted in a drill press really is needed to construct it with any efficiency. It could be done with hand tools, but it would be a lot of work.

The starting point is three or four strips each of the chosen timbers. Maple is commonly used for the lighter coloured wood and here Peruvian walnut or Tasmanian blackwood have been used for the contrasting strips. The thickness of the strips is the length of each element of the binding once it is all put together so they could be anywhere from 3mm/⅛" to 6mm/¼" depending on the look you want to achieve. The exact thickness of each strip is not important, as long as they are consistent. 4mm/5⁄32" looks about right on a ukulele. For a Weissenborn style guitar thicker strips might look better.

The strips start out 5cm/2" wide and 60cm/24" long which will allow a 'loaf' to be glued up about the same length from which the binding strips will be cut. A 60cm/24" strip will be enough for one side of a

The strips of alternate coloured timber ready to be glued.

The block glued and clamped in the simple fixture with the angled block at one end.

Below: The laminated block with the edges cleaned up of any glue squeeze-out and machined square.

Angled blocks being cut from the larger laminated block.

The small angled blocks being rub-glued together into another block which will be the length of each binding strip.

Below: The veneer which will be the inside border of each binding strip glued to opposite sides of the block.

baritone ukulele body. The strips are glued together, alternating the colours, in a simple fixture made from two pieces of 7.5cm/3″ wide melamine faced MDF. At one end is a block of wood sliced at a 40° angle. The glue used is a more heat and moisture resistant glue such as Titebond III or another exterior-grade cross-linked PVA. Cling film is used to stop the glued block getting stuck to the fixture. Let this dry overnight.

Rope binding need not be simple alternating colours of the same size blocks. Thinner strips of a third colour can be interleaved or a sparser look can be done with single coloured strips alternated with a contrasting veneer.

When fully dry, clean up the edges of glue squeeze-out and run the block through the sander to get a smooth surface on the sides showing the laminations. If necessary, clean up any glue from the top and bottom strips. Mark a line on one of the faces showing the laminations at a 40° angle on one end and trim that off. Cut the rest of the laminated block into 4cm/1½″ sections following the 40° angle. A piece of 18mm/¾″ plywood cut and sanded to a 40° angle indexes off the saw fence as an improvised guide. The length of the sections does not really matter, as long as they are of a consistent length. You should end up with six or seven blocks. Sand the newly sawn edges to get rid of any saw fuzz.

Glue these small blocks together on the gluing fixture using the 40° angled piece of timber as a stop at one end (if needed). Trying to clamp several angled blocks slippery with glue at one time is difficult, and it is easier to use a simple rubbed joint on two of them at a time and then join the double blocks after the glue has set. The finished block will have the laminations running vertically on one face and at a 40° angle on the adjacent faces. Again, leave overnight for the glue to fully dry, then smooth each surface by several light passes through the thickness sander. By this stage there are a lot of glued surfaces and it is worthwhile being gentle.

Glue a piece of veneer (matching one of the timbers, in this case plain maple) to two opposite sides of the block. If the veneer is glued to the surface

Sawing a strip off each of the veneer-faced sides of the block.

Cleaning up the sawn binding strips before final machining to set the depth of the binding.

with vertical rather than angled laminations, it means that when the finished binding strips are glued into the binding rebates on the body, the angled sections are visible looking down on the body. If the veneer is glued to the angled side of the block, the blocks are rectangular when looked at from above. In the end this does not really matter because the rope effect appears when the bindings are rounded over.

A couple of pieces of offcut MDF with waxed paper are used as cauls to apply even pressure to the veneer from several big clamps. The veneer may want to absorb moisture and warp, so this should also be left overnight to dry.

This veneer will become the purfling strip inside the rope binding, which also helps keep the binding together when bending it. Once the glue has dried slice off a 4mm/0.160" strip and sand to 3mm/0.120" thick. With the 0.7mm/0.028" veneer this gives 2.3mm of binding. On a ukulele the binding looks right when it is around 2mm/0.080" wide, plus the veneer purfling. A 2.3mm/0.090" width allows a little leeway. Glue another piece of veneer on the just machined face. This will be sacrificed by being sanded away once the binding is fitted, but again helps keep the strip together when bending. This "sacrificial" layer could just as easily be a slice of cheap softwood, sawn and glued as a thicker layer and then machined down

The sawn strips have been machined to what will be the final width of the binding. A sacrificial veneer glued to the second face before the individual binding strips are cut a little oversize.

Final thicknessing in the drum sander.

to 0.5-0.7mm thick. Alternatively it could be cut from the other timber used for the rope (if no commercial veneer was available) so there is the option of using either colour for the purfling strip and sanding the other away.

The rope binding will look in proportion at around 2.5-3mm/0.100-0.120" deep. Slice strips 3.5-4mm/0.140-0.160" wide from the veneered pieces, sanding smooth the edge that indexes from the fence before each cut. Yet again run them through the thickness sander to the final height required.

The process can be repeated by smoothing the sawn faces of the master block, gluing veneer, slicing off, veneering and cutting into binding strips.

The binding strips can be bent quite successfully in the small Fox side bender, wrapped in damp paper towel and aluminium foil. The strips should be gently pressed into shape over the form using a temperature of around 140°C/280°F for five minutes. Too much heat and moisture and the binding strips start to revert to their individual components. There might also be some compression of the width of the strip around the waist, where the waist caul pushes the strips into the waist area of the form. Measure the width of the strips in the waist area. Use that as the width of the body rebate if that measurement is less than that at the widest parts of the bouts, where any compression would be minimal.

Binding strips ready for bending.

Above: Three binding/purfling cutters. From the left; a Schnieder gramil, an Ibex and a shop made version from maple.

Above: The LMI routerbase for cutting the binding ledge. The instrument needs to be held horizontally in a cradle and the router base is free to move vertically.

Below: The router cutter with differently sized bearings to determine the width of the rebate.

CUTTING THE BINDING REBATE

Whatever style of binding is used, a rebate or ledge needs to be cut to the depth and width of the binding plus whatever purfling might be used. If rope binding is used the rebate should be the minimum width of the bent strip excluding the outside veneer. This will usually be around 2.5-3mm/0.100-0.120" in each direction.

The rebate can be hand cut with a purfling cutter or a dedicated router setup. Both Luthiers Mercantile and Stewart-MacDonald offer router jigs for this purpose and designs for similar jigs are freely available.

A hand cutter, to score the bottom and inside edges of the rebate, can be made from timber off-cuts and a small blade or there are several commercial types available. The Schneider gramil is a useful tool for this procedure.

The cutter is used to score the lines taking care to hold the device firmly to the body and not tilt it as the cut is made. A sharp chisel removes the waste and another shallow cut is made. Once the required size of the rebate ledge is reached check with the bindings for fit. Smooth out the curves and any lumps with a file and a chisel used as a scraper. The binding needs to fit as neatly in the rebate as possible.

If an integral neck ukulele is being built it is usual for the bindings to continue under the end of the fretboard. Neither a router or a hand cutter will cut the blind slot needed. A sharp knife and a narrow chisel will be needed to cut the slot around 5mm/3/16" long. A suitable narrow chisel may need to be made from a piece of hard steel, such as a hacksaw blade.

A similar approach may be needed for binding around the back, depending on the type of construction. If the back extends over and is glued to the back of the heel of an integral neck ukulele, the binding may be cut at an angle to stop just inside the line of the heel.

INSTALLING BINDING

The gluing process should start at the neck end of the body. The fretboard will cover the ends and the binding and purfling should be progressively glued and taped into place. Wooden binding should meet at the tail preferably using a mitred join. One side should be done and the miter cut at the tail. The second side can then be glued with the the miter carefully cut before gluing the last 40-50mm/2".

Plastic binding, whether celluloid or another plastic such as ABS, can be purchased in lengths long enough to easily go around a ukulele body. This saves having to worry about a neat mitered join at the tail.

The gluing is best done in short sections of 75-100mm/3-4". A bead of glue is applied to the rebate ledge and a thin layer of glue is applied to one side of any purfling. The aim is to have a small amount of glue on every surface to be glued.

For solid wooden binding aliphatic resin or hot hide glue can be used, but the short open time of the hide glue may well require a heat source, such as a heated heavy metal spatula to soften the glue and allow the binding to be pulled into place by the tape. The aliphatic resin glues have a longer open time, but any squeeze-out in the grain of the surrounding timber can be visible under a finish.

If required, plastic and celluloid binding can be pre-bent in hot water or with a hot air gun, ***taking care not to set it alight***. Most plastic binding is flexible enough to simply glue into place. An acetone-based solvent glue, as used in the acrylic industry, is used to glue the binding and purfling.

Using a mixture of wooden and plastic binding or purfling can complicate the gluing process. The acetone-based cements will work with wood if necessary. Some builders use aliphatic resin to glue celluloid, brushing the celluloid with acetone to slightly soften the surface, then getting the binding taped into place within a short window before the acetone evaporates. Make sure the work area is well ventilated.

The binding around the back of the baritone ukulele let into the heel cap.

Above: Using a gramil to cut the rebate.

Below: A sharp chisel and a file are used to refine the rebate.

GLUING ROPE BINDING

If possible, hot animal glue should be used to glue the rope binding strips. The heat and moisture will soften the strips a little as they are taped into place and help bed them into the sides of the rebate. A heated heavy spatula or even a clothes iron can be used to further encourage the binding into position.

Leave the taped binding to fully dry overnight. Small gaps can usually be filled by application of more heat from the spatula or clothes iron to push the strips into closer contact.

Once fully dry and as gap-free as possible the binding can be trimmed with a scraper and/or sandpaper. If everything has gone well it should only be the sacrificial layer of veneer on the outside which will need to be removed and the binding should be flush with the sides. If not, either the binding will have to be narrowed or the sides thinned to be flush with the binding. This must be done with care as the sides will only be 1.5-2mm/0.060-0.080" thick.

Rope binding can then be rounded over with sandpaper to a quarter-circle cross-section. This means the angled joins can be seen from all directions.

Pre-bent rope binding strips glued with hot hide glue and taped into place. A clothes iron is used to remelt the glue slightly and push the binding flush.

CHAPTER 9
SOPRANO UKULELE

The early Hawaiian-made ukuleles used an integral neck construction, as shown in a 1917 short film on ukulele building made by the Ford Motor Company, and described in **Chapter 12.** When mass production of ukuleles began in the mid-1910s the Chicago and East Coast factories in the United States adapted guitar building techniques to ukuleles. This included making the neck and body separately and bringing them together as one of the last stages of the building process. A common neck attachment for American guitars was a tapered dovetail joint, which can be made accurately and repeatably with jigs and power driven cutters. The lower string tension of a ukulele does mean that a simpler joining process can be used. For this soprano ukulele the neck is glued into a shallow mortice in the same way that a violin neck is attached.

This chapter describes the assembly of a soprano ukulele modelled, at least in its general shape, on a Regal instrument of the 1920s. The neck and body are made separately, with the neck glued into place before the back is glued. This methodology can be used for any size of ukulele, with the size of the body mould adjusted to suit the size of the instrument. Three instruments were built, one from an Australian native timber, Tulip satinwood (R*hodosphaera rhodanthema*), another from Monkeypod (*Samanea saman*) and the third from Australian blackwood (*Acacia melanoxylon*) and the illustrations are from the construction of all of these instruments.

An outside mould should be made following the directions in **Chapter 3.** The basic processes of neck construction are covered in **Chapter 6,** which covers the marking out of the neck profile on the neck blank and the shaping of the head. The soundboard and back should be constructed as directed in **Chapter 4** and the sides bent into shape as per **Chapter 5.**

BENDING THE SIDES

For this soprano ukulele the sides were shaped in the Fox side bender. They were bent from timber 60mm/2⅜″ wide and 1.5mm/0.060″ thick. Once the heat blanket was up to temperature the sides were pulled into shape and cooked for four minutes at 150°C/300°F. The temperature was reduced to 100°C/212°F and left for another 10 minutes. The blanket was then turned off and the sides allowed to cool. Those temperatures are approximate and are from the markings on the controller supplied with the heat blanket. Different timbers might require different temperatures and times.

Triangular cross-section kerfed linings were used for these ukuleles. These were made from a softwood, Pacific kauri, but a light hardwood such as basswood or poplar could be substituted. Pre-made kerfed linings are available in sizes suitable for a ukulele from the main lutherie supply houses.

A tailblock being laminated from three pieces of spruce, the grain of the thinner centre laminate at a right angle to the other two.

THE TAILBLOCK & NECKBLOCK

A laminated tailblock should be made following the direction in **Chapter 5**. For this soprano ukulele the block will be 5cm/2" wide, 5.5cm/2³⁄₁₆" high (a little longer than the sides are wide to allow trimming) and 13mm/½" thick. One side needs to be shaped to follow the curvature of the end of the mould. This can be done on a disk sander or by hand with a plane and sandpaper. The grain of the shaped side should follow the grain of the sides with the endgrain of the centre lamination visible on the top and bottom. Mark a vertical centreline all around.

The neck block is a piece of light-medium density hardwood such as mahogany 50mm/2" wide, 18mm/¾" thick and 50mm/2" high to allow for the tapering of the sides to a height of 47mm/1⅞" at the neck join. The grain follows that of the sides so there is no endgrain gluing. The glued-in neck will help re-enforce the block against splits. The front edge is shaped to fit the curve of the sides in the same way as the tailblock.

Marking the lengths of a side in the mould so the two sides meet cleanly on the centreline at each end. Extra clamps may be used to pull the sides into the mould.

Above: One large G-clamp is used to glue each block, with two spring clamps to glue the tailblock where it is above of the mould.

Below: The front curve of the neckblock being shaped on a disc sander.

Below: The neckblock glued in the same way.

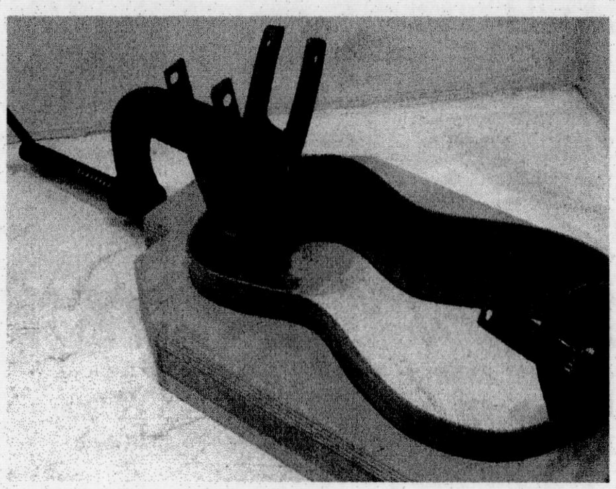

THE SIDE ASSEMBLY

Cut the sides to length so they are seated firmly in the mould and the ends butt up evenly where the mould halves join. A strip of masking tape over the join on the outside will stop glue leakage though the join. This can otherwise adhere the sides to the mould itself when the blocks are glued and clamped in place. The mould should be placed on a flat surface (such as the workbench or auxiliary workboard) with a layer of clingwrap or similar to stop everything becoming glued to that surface, with what will be the edges that will be glued to the soundboard pushed down the flat surface. The sides should protrude 6-10mm/¼-⅜" depending on how the mould was made.

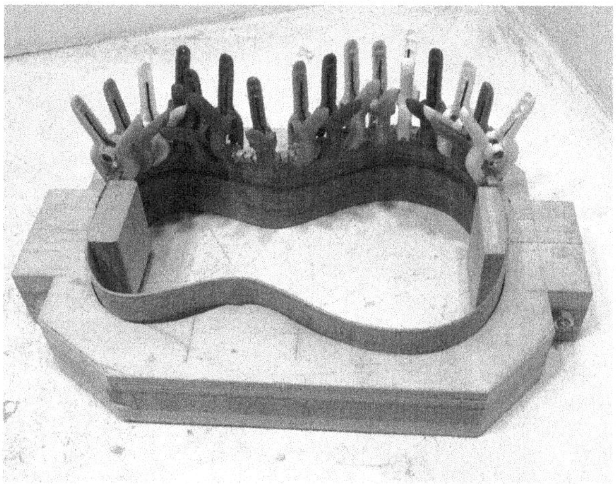

Gluing one side of the linings on the soundboard edge of the sides.

Smear glue on the curved faces of each block, lining up the marked centrelines to the join of the mould halves. Clamp them into position ensuring that the bottom of each block is sitting on the supporting flat surface. The tail block can be held to the protruding sides by a couple of spring clamps if required.

Above: Leveling the linings with a finely set block plane.

Once the glue is dry remove the clamps and loosen the mould so the sides and block assembly can be pushed through so the soundboard edge protrudes. Fit and glue the kerfed soundboard linings so they protrude above the sides by around .5mm/1⁄32". Leave this overnight before removing the clamps and plane or sand the linings flush with the sides. Keep the side and block assembly firmly clamped in the mould. A few large spring clamps can be used to hold the sides in place if spreader blocks have not been fitted. This will ensure that the finished side/lining surface is in the one plane. It is quite easy to sand a dip into the waist area if the side/block assembly is allowed to flex when the levelling is done.

Below: Sanding the linings on a large sanding board, a piece of melamine covered MDF with strips of 80-grit sandpaper glued to it.

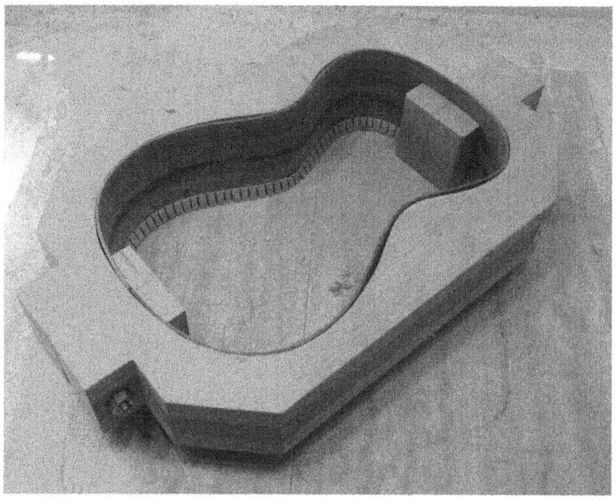

A large flat sanding board, a piece of melamine-faced MDF the size of at least two sheets of sandpaper, with strips or sheets of 80-grit sandpaper glued to it is useful to flatten the entire surface. The one used here is 50cm x 40cm/20" x16", 40cm/16" being the width of four strips of 80-grit sandpaper from a roll.

Trimming the width of the sides to the required end to end taper.

Above: Using the large sanding board to finish the tapering.

Below: A side view of the side taper.

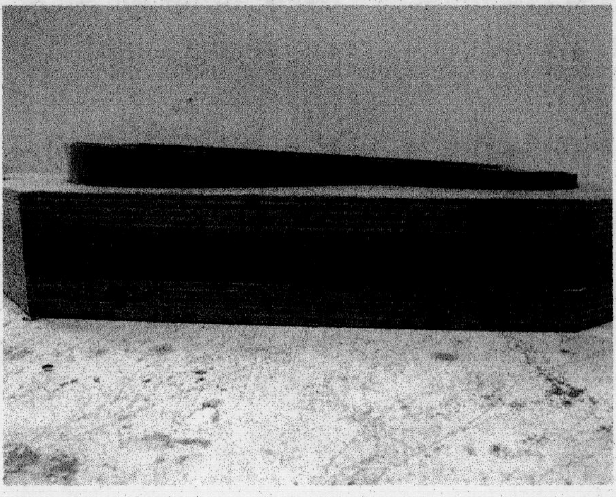

THE SIDE TAPER

The next procedure is to shape the bottom edges of the sides so the depth of the body tapers from the tailblock to the neck join. This small ukulele uses a straight taper from tail to neck, with a transverse curve forced onto the back from the single transverse back brace. The slightest of bevels can be sanded into the edge of the sides and the linings for a clean glue join to the back.

The sides are only 1.5-2mm/0.060-0.080" thick and will cut easily with a sharp chisel or a block plane. At the same time they are fragile and care must be taken to prevent splitting along the grain.

On the outside, mark the desired finished height of the neck and tail blocks - 48mm/1⅞" and 58mm/1⁵⁄₁₆". Replace the side assembly back in the mould and push it through so the back edges of the sides protrude. The side assembly must protrude enough so the bottom of the neck block can be shaped to follow the body taper. It can be useful to use four small blocks of timber or plywood of the same thickness. These are placed inside the mould under the neck and tailbacks and the waist to ensure the sides are sitting square and evenly protruding.

Chisel or plane the sides carefully, sighting down the body to check the line of the trimming and measure the depth of the sides at opposite points to ensure symmetry.

The back of the neck block will end up a couple of millimetres higher than the front (where it is glued to the sides) because of the body taper. Again, a large sanding board is very useful to refine the entire plane of the back edge of the sides.

Glue and level the back linings in the same way as was done for the linings on the soundboard edges. A smaller sanding block can be used to sand a small bevel to account for the transverse curvature of the back induced by the single brace.

GLUING THE SOUNDBOARD

The side assembly can be left in the mould for the fitting of the soundboard and back to ensure it stays in shape.

Place the soundboard facedown on the bench or workboard with the side assembly on top. Line up the centrelines on both neck and tail blocks with the centreline marked on the inside of the soundboard. Use a pencil to mark on both where the linings meet the two transverse braces. Check that the height of the braces at that point is 3mm/⅛″ and adjust that if necessary. Trim the length of the braces so they extend halfway into the linings and cut notches 3mm/⅛″ deep in the linings to suit. There should be a gap of around 1mm/1⁄32″ between the ends of the braces and the back of the notch. This gives a little adjustment room when gluing the soundboard to the sides. Make sure the notches are deep enough for the linings and blocks to sit evenly on the soundboard.

Repeat the process to fit the back and set the back aside until the neck is fitted.

The soundboard should now be glued to the sides using whatever kind of clamps are available. Run a thin line of glue around the linings and blocks and bring together. Clamp the neck and tail blocks first, taking care to keep them square to the soundboard. This is to ensure that the gluing surfaces meet as exactly as possible and add more clamps gently. Over-tightening the clamps can pull the sides out of square and not much clamping pressure is needed to hold the flat plane of the sides to the flat soundboard. Any squeeze-out on the inside can be cleaned up with a damp cloth or paper towel. Once the glue is dry trim back any overhang of the soundboard with a chisel or sanding block.

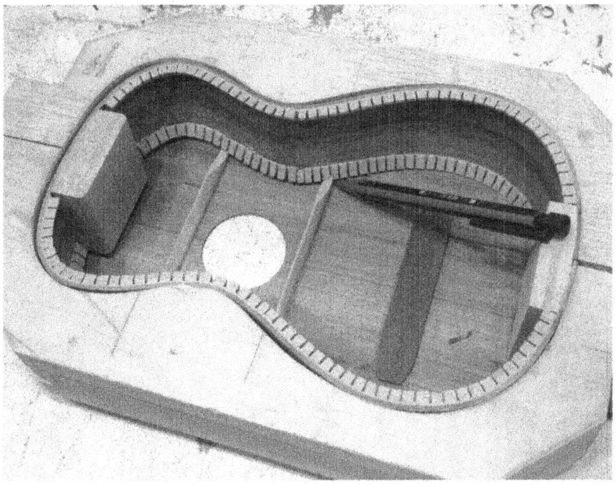

Marking the linings for notches to clear the soundboard braces.

Gluing the sides to the soundboard which is face down on a solera workboard.

Trimming the heel to the marked taper.

Above: Checking the straightness of the taper.

Below: The finished heel, matching the width of the fretboard at the 12th fret.

Marking the heel shape on the end of the body.

Above: The body mortice cut to match the heel taper.

Below: Gluing the neck in place with the acrylic line-up jig, with large rubber bands holding the neck in place.

FITTING A GLUED-IN NECK

This neck is made with a straight tapering heel which is glued directly into a similarly shaped mortice in the ukulele body. The heel tapers from 45mm/1⅞" wide under the 12th fret to 15mm/⅝" wide where it meets the back. The neck should be cut to length, allowing the 6mm/¼" extra length of the heel where it extends into the mortice. Sand the end smooth to 120-grit.

Trim the heel depth to around 1mm more than the width of the sides (which should be close to 48mm/1⅞") at the neckblock. Mark the centreline on the back of the heel and the 15mm/⅝" width of the bottom of the heel. To keep the geometry of the mortice as simple as possible the sides of the tapered heel are kept parallel to the centreline of the neck. The greatest width is the width of the fretboard at the 12th fret (which should be 45mm/1¾") tapering down to 15mm/⅝". This will hide the mortice under the fretboard a little more effectively than if the extension follows the fretboard width.

Fit the fretboard to the neck with pins as described in **Chapter 7** and mark the fretboard width at the 12th fret. Remove the fretboard and draw lines parallel to the centreline on either side at that width from the end of the neck to the point where the heel starts to flare. Make saw cuts at that point from the edge of the neck blank almost to the marked lines.

Hold the neck in a vice while shaping the heel taper. Gradually cut away the excess, taking care to keep the taper straight as well as parallel to the centreline.

The fretboard should be used to check the final width of the heel top and a 150mm/6" machinist's ruler is useful for ensuring that the taper is straight. Sand smooth to 120-grit once the final shape is established.

A matching mortice is cut into the end of the body. Mark the shape, score with a sharp knife and cut to to just inside the lines with a razor saw allowing .5mm/1⁄32" or so for final enlarging of the mortice. A sharp chisel and sanding sticks are used to refine the mortice until the neck extension is a gentle press fit in all three axes.

Scott Wise's jig for cutting the body mortice with a router.

Above: Gluing the back with rubber bands and a clamp over the neck block.

A rigid piece of 6mm/¼" acrylic with a scribed centreline is used as a jig to keep the neck in alignment while being glued into the mortice. A couple of large rubber bands or rope is used to pull the neck into the mortice while the glue dries and various clamps are used to hold the neck and body to the alignment jig. Any glue squeeze-out should be removed before it dries.

Instead of hand cutting the heel and the mortice, a router jig can be set up to cut the mortice, with a matching bandsaw jig to shape the neck heel.

Illustrated on the previous page is Scott Wise's simple but effective router jig for a ball-bearing flush-cut router bit. The sides and soundboard assembly is fixed to the jig with the wooden bar clamped through the soundhole and the router cuts a correctly sized mortice. A tilting jig for the bandsaw cuts the heel taper almost to size. The sawn heel is cleaned up to match the mortice and glued into place.

The bottom of the heel should be trimmed to the taper of the sides and the back glued in place. The back brace should fit neatly into the notches cut into the back linings. Large rubber bands are used to clamp the back in place. The instrument is placed facedown on a ukulele shaped workboard with slots or wood screws around the edge and the rubber bands used to apply clamping pressure. An alternative method uses a couple of wooden cam clamps for the blocks and shop-made spool clamps around the perimeter. This is illustrated in **Chapter 11** in assembling a tenor ukulele.

Once dry, trim the overhang and fit the binding and purfling, if used, as described in **Chapter 8**.

The body can now be sanded to at least 180-grit, and 240-grit on a softwood soundboard.

GLUING THE FRETBOARD

The fretboard, with all but two frets installed, should now be glued to the neck, either with epoxy or wood glue. A caul should be made from 12mm/½" plywood with holes drilled to clear to two locating nails. The caul should be a millimetre or two slightly narrower than the fretboard itself. A strip of 3mm/⅛" wide veneer should be glued along each edge to add more clamping pressure to the edges of the fretboard, especially if a slight arch was sanded across the board.

It can be useful to sand the neck surface lightly with a half-sheet sanding board to remove any surface oxidation of the wood before brushing or blowing any dust clear. Wipe down the underneath surface of the fretboard itself with acetone to ensure it is clean of any oils. This is important if a rosewood fingerboard is used.

A fretboard being glued with a plywood caul to even the clamping pressure. The small hole visible in the caul is to clear one of the locating pins.

Apply the glue, fit the nails through the fret slots and into the neck and clamp in place with the caul. Carefully clean up any squeeze-out around the back of the heel and the extension tongue as any dollops of dried glue will interfere with the neck fit. Similarly clean the nut slot of any squeeze-out. Leave to dry overnight before removing the clamps, cleaning out the two empty fret slots and installing the last two frets.

Trim the width of the neck to that of the fretboard, cleaning up any glue squeezout along the edges of the fretboard. The final shape of the neck shaft can now be carved. That is described in **Chapter 13**.

Making and fitting a bridge is described in **Chapter 14**. If a wipe-on oil finish is used the bridge can be glued in place before the finish is applied. If a sprayed lacquer finish is to be used the bridge should be glued in place after the final buffing of the lacquer. **Chapter 16** deals with the options for finishing the ukulele.

CHAPTER 10

CONCERT & BARITONE UKULELE

BUILDING A UKULELE IN THE SPANISH STYLE

Ukuleles built in this way are assembled face down on a *solera* workboard using the same basic methodology as traditional Spanish classical guitar makers. Information is given in **Chapter 3** on making appropriately sized workboards.

A solera workboard for a concert sized ukulele.

A larger solera workboard for a baritone ukulele, with more slots for the dowel supports and wood screws in the edges for rubber bands to attach to when gluing the back.

Most of the photos in this chapter deal with the assembly of a concert sized ukulele, while others were taken during the construction of a baritone sized instrument. The principals are the same, just the size varies.

The workboard should be fixed in a vice, preferably a bench-mounted vice that rotates (such as a Versa-Vice, the Parrot Vice from LMI or Stewart-MacDonald's Luthier's Vice) so it is accessible from all sides. Alternatively, it can be held in a normal bench vice and cantilevered out from the bench.

SPANISH HEEL SIDE SLOTS

In this style of construction the sides fit into slots cut into each side of the heel section of the neck. It does not matter if the neck is to be cut from a solid block, a laminated blank or built-up from thinner timber, the process is the same.

The slots need to be the same width as the thickness of the sides, and because the body outline curves into the neck these slots must be cut at a 5° angle. They are cut to within 3-4mm/⅛-5/32" of the centreline. The slots may be cut on a table saw, a bandsaw, or with a handsaw using an angled block of wood as a guide. If cut with a handsaw, a second cut may be necessary to achieve the correct width. A metal scraper can be used as a spacer. Mark the 45mm/1¾" width of the fretboard at the 12th fret position on the top surface of the neck. The front of the slots should meet the 12th fret position at that point (the 14th fret for a 14 fret tenor or baritone).

SHAPING THE NECK

Before the neck is glued to the soundboard the head should be cut to shape and final thickness, the heel shaped and tapered, and the width of the neck reduced to the tapered profile of the fretboard.

The head should have the overlay veneer (if used) glued in place, the head outline cut to size, the head thickness tapered and at least pilot holes for the tuners as described in **Chapter 6**.

The width of the neck can now be refined to 35mm/1⅜" wide at the nut widening out to 45mm/1⅞" at the 12th fret position. The safest way

The concert size neck cut close to the width of the fretboard. The head has also been shaped and thicknessed with pilot holes drilled for the tuners.

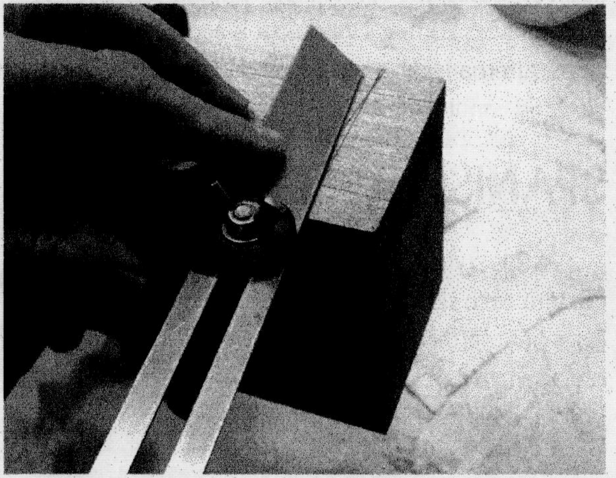

Marking the 5° angle of the slots on to the top surface of the neck.

The baritone heel carved and rough sanded.

A saw square with a 5° guide block attached.

The heel of the concert ukulele with the sides inserted into the slots.

to do this is to clamp the shaped but unfretted fingerboard to the neck in its correct position, using a couple of spring clamps. Two small holes can be drilled through the 2nd and 11th fret slots around 5mm/3⁄16" into the neck itself. Typical ukulele fretwire is around 1.3mm/0.053" wide so a couple of 1mm brad point nails make suitable pins.

The fretboard will act as a template to mark the width the neck and the waste can be chiseled away, or carefully cut off with a saw. Trim the neck width to that of the fretboard, keeping the rectangular cross-section for the moment. This makes it easier to hold the assembled instrument in a vice for procedures such as fitting the binding. It is easier to carve the neck shape after the fretboard is glued into place.

Before the soundboard and the sides are attached to the neck the heel should be tapered and carved to the final shape. The heel usually tapers from the width of the fretboard to 10-15mm/3⁄8-5⁄8" wide where it meets the back. Most ukuleles use a straight taper in width rather than the curves of a classical guitar. The bottom of the heel should be shaped to a point at the front edge of the heel and the rest of the heel at least roughly carved. The important thing at this stage is to have the sides of the heel shaped before the sides are fitted into their slots.

Trying to shape and sand smooth the edges of the heel after the sides are fixed into the neck slots is harder than when the neck is still separate, and will avoid noticeable cross-grain sanding scratches in the sides where they meet the neck.

CUTTING THE SOUNDBOARD LEDGE

The extension of the neck into the body should be trimmed to 50mm/2" wide. Sand smooth and bevel or round over the inside vertical edges. The exposed end-grain on the inside can be sealed with a wash of shellac, superglue or thinned epoxy as an insurance against cracking, though this is optional.

Marking the depth of the ledge by holding the soundboard to the heel extension.

The ledge ready for gluing to the soundboard.

The concert ukulele soundboard centred and clamped to the solera workboard.

The baritone neck glued and clamped to the soundboard.

Place the neck upside down on a smooth surface and mark the thickness of the soundboard on the neck extension. When assembling the ukulele the neck extension must fit exactly over and be glued to the soundboard to ensure the structural integrity of the entire instrument. Carefully chisel away the ledge and check the fit.

GLUING THE NECK TO THE SOUNDBOARD

The next step is gluing the soundboard to the neck. The section of the neck that extends into the body should have a ledge cut on the top surface exactly the thickness of the soundboard. Clamp the soundboard to the workboard with a small piece of timber that spans the two transverse braces (or one that fits across the soundhole) and held in place by a bolt that engages the T-nut installed on the bottom of the workboard under the position of the soundhole. Take care that the centreline is aligned with the workboard centreline.

NOTE: *If building a baritone ukulele with a slightly arched soundboard remember to keep the card spacer in place around the edge of the soundboard as described in **Chapter 4**.*

Test fit the neck. The soundboard gluing ledge should just touch the soundboard when the top surface is held firmly to the workboard. Make sure the centreline of the neck is clearly marked on the top/fretboard surface and the inside face of the body extension. Align the neck centreline with that marked on the inside of the soundboard and the line on the end of the workboard and clamped in place (this will involve checking from underneath the workboard). Two small blocks of wood can be tack-glued to the workboard at the nut end of the workboard to help align the neck.

Take off the clamps, apply a thin coat of glue to the ledge and re-clamp the soundboard. Check again before the glue grabs that the centrelines all line up. Make sure no glue has squeezed into the slots in the neck where the sides will be inserted.

THE TAILBLOCK

The tailblock can be made from a single piece of wood such as spruce or mahogany, remembering that if the grain of the block follows that of the sides an impact can split the block, and if the grain is perpendicular to the sides, that soundboard and back are glued to end-grain.

A lightweight and strong tailblock can be made from three laminated pieces of thick spruce or other softwood as described in **Chapter 5**. The outside laminates have their grain direction following that of the sides, with the centre lamination at 90°. This lessens the chance of the tailblock splitting if the instrument gets dropped and at the same time minimises end-grain gluing.

Marking the tail end of one of the baritone sides.

The tailblocks are 5cm/2" wide and made as high as is required for the different sizes of ukulele. Always allow another 3mm/⅛" for the doming of the back. Glue up the blocks a little oversize and cut or sand to the finished dimensions. One surface need to be shaped to the curve of the end of the ukulele. This can be done by hand with a small plane and sanding blocks, or on a disc sander. Check that it matches the shape of the tailblock caul. The curved side needs to be precisely at 90° to the edge that will be glued to the soundboard. Mark a centreline with a pencil on all four surfaces.

GLUING THE SIDES & TAILBLOCK

Remove the neck/soundboard assembly from the workboard. Fit the dowel side supports and the tail caul firmly to the workboard, following the soundboard outline. The sides need to be trimmed to length, fitting closely at the tail join if a tail graft is not used. Spring clamps can be used to hold the over-length sides to the dowels and the sides marked where they cross the centreline at the tail and 3mm/⅛" out from the centreline at the neck end. This allows for the web between the two slots. Use a small engineer's square to make a line from the soundboard edge of the sides. That is the edge which will sit flat on the soundboard and so the two sides will meet neatly at the tail. If the sides have not been bent as precisely as they could have been, it can be worthwhile to leave an extra millimetre or so in the first trimming of the sides' length and gradually trim to an exact fit.

Replace the neck/soundboard assembly and test fit the sides in the neck slots and the way they follow the body outline (touching all the dowels) to meet at the tail. The sides should fit into the neck slots without being forced. They should be touching the soundboard along their whole length and closely following the outline. The sides should fit neatly between the dowels and the ends of the transverse braces. Again spring clamps are useful to pull recalcitrant sides into proper alignment. The sides should meet neatly at the tail, on the centreline and fit closely, without forcing, into the neck slots. They can be a little shorter if necessary, as long as they are not too short and expose a gap at the bottom of the heel.

Gluing the tailblock on the baritone. Two clamps hold the tailblock to the caul and the third maintains downward pressure to the soundboard.

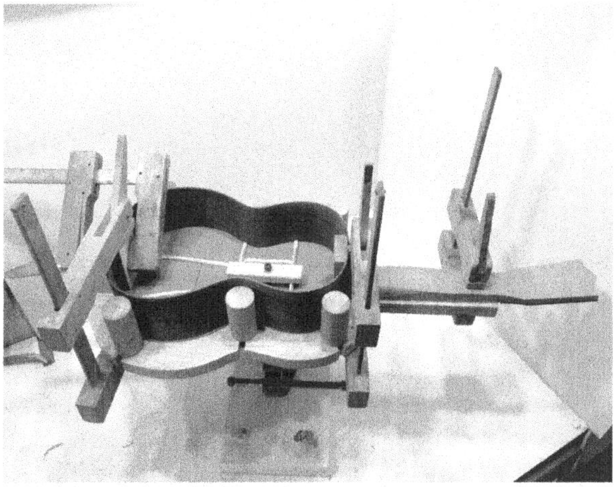

Gluing the tailblock on the concert ukulele. The clamps on the neck make sure that the soundboard and neck are in the one plane.

Tape the tail ends of the sides closely together with a strip of masking tape on the outside. This will prevent any excess glue attaching the sides to the caul. Smear glue onto the last 12mm/½" of the inside surface of the neck end of the sides and insert into the neck slots. Check that the lower edge of both sides contact the soundboard along their length. Spring or cam-clamps can be used to ensure that contact.

Cutting the tentallones in a model-maker's mitre box.

Above: Tentallones being glued between the soundboard and a side.

Below: The concert ukulele with the tentallones glued in place.

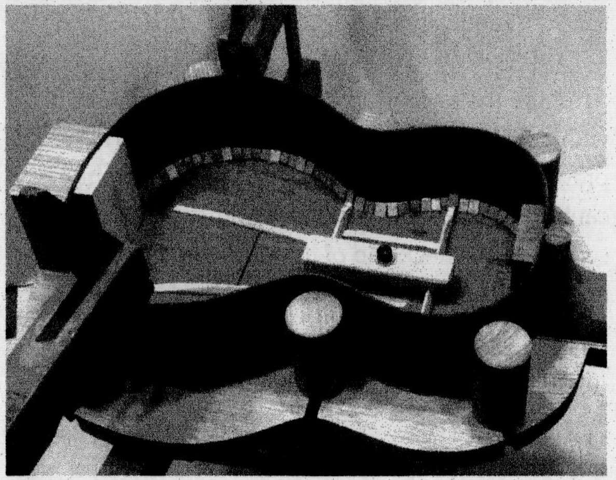

Apply glue to the back and top edges of the tailblock and clamp into place. One clamp, or perhaps two small ones, pulls the tailblock into the caul, while another maintains downwards pressure onto the soundboard. The tailblock needs to be firmly glued to the soundboard as well as the sides or it will compromise the structural integrity of the instrument.

It is worthwhile to practice this part of the assembly process a couple of times without any glue involved.

TENTALLONES

The sides are held to the soundboard by gluing small triangular pieces of softwood - *tentallones* - around the inside. These are made from strips of timber machined to 5 x 7mm /3/16" x 9/32" then planed to a triangular cross section. The triangular strips are then cut into 5-6mm/3/16-1/4" lengths with a razor saw and hobbyist's miter-box. They are rub-glued into position, trimming and bevelling as necessary to fit around the transverse braces, with four tentallones gluing the ends of the braces to the sides. Hide glue is preferable for this process, but aliphatic can be used. Leave overnight to dry.

SHAPING THE SIDE PROFILE

The sides have to be shaped to the tapered depth of the body. The sides are only 1.5-2mm/0.060-0.080" thick and will cut easily with a sharp chisel. At the same time they are fragile and care must be taken to prevent splitting along the grain. It is safer to shape the sides after they are firmly anchored to the soundboard, neck and tail block.

The simplest approach is to have a straight taper from tail to neck, with a slight transverse curve from one or two back braces. A slight bevel needs to be sanded into the edge of the sides and the linings for a neat glue join to the back. This is an old Spanish guitar building methodology, now out of fashion.

A more sophisticated approach is using a concave sanding dish to shape the sides, the neck extension and the tail block into a section of a sphere. The section in **Chapter 3** on **Workboards** describes the construction of a concave sanding dish and the mounting of an axle in a solera workboard.

Start by marking the final desired height of the sides at the tail and the neck join. Refer to the plans for measurements. If using the sandpaper lined dished workboard to shape the sides, also mark the tail measurement at the waist, as the sides around the almost circular lower bout will stay at much the same height. This will be a useful starting point for the shaping with the sanding dish.

Doming the side profile of the baritone ukulele with the dished workboard. The metal tube that acts as an axle can be seen protruding through the centre of the dish.

With a chisel or a block plane, trim the sides down almost to the final height. Also trim the tailblock and neck extension at the same time. The straight taper can be refined with a half sheet sanding board or a larger sanding board (also as described in ***Chapter 3***) can be used to sand the sides and the blocks in one plane.

With the dished sanding board the profile of the sides is a little more complex. They will stay more-or-less the same height from the tail to the waist and then dip down to the neck join. The depth at the heel will be slightly greater than at the widest parts of the upper bout because of the transverse arch sanded in by the dish.

Above: Gluing solid back linings. The hole for the sanding dish axle can be seen through the soundhole.

The critical thing to remember when using the dish is to check very regularly to keep the sanding even on both sides. It is remarkably easy to sand one side (especially on the widest part of the lower bout) noticeably more than the other. A line of chalk on the edges is useful for identifying low points.

Below: The back linings glued and sanded level with the dished workboard. The axle is in place for the radiused sanding dish.

BACK LININGS

The sides should be sanded to within a 0.5-1mm/1⁄32″ of the final height, taking care to sand evenly so opposite points on the sides are the same height. Back linings need to be fitted to add rigidity to the structure and provide more gluing surface for the back than the sides alone would provide. These can be either solid or kerfed linings as described in **Chapter 5**. The tight curves of small ukuleles can provide a challenge to get kerfed strips glued in

Notches cut into the back linings to accept the back braces.

without breaking into shorter lengths, but it makes little practical difference if the linings are in one piece or four.

For both the concert and baritone ukuleles built for this chapter solid linings were used and bent in the same way as the sides. They were held in place with just a few clamps and trimmed to fit neatly between the neck and tail blocks. Glue in place with lots of small clamps leaving around 1mm above the level of the sides. If the sides were shaped with the dished sanding board a little bending and twisting as they are glued will be needed to keep them even with the side profile.

FITTING THE BACK

Sand the sides and linings down to the final height, checking for evenness and that the gluing surface is smooth and continuous. This is especially

The back glued into place with large rubber bands.

important if there is no binding on the back join. Shake and vacuum all the dust and shavings out. Mark the centreline on the front of the heel and position the back in place with a couple of rubber bands or spool clamps. The centreline on the heel, the back and the tail join should all line up. The position of the back braces can be marked on the sides with a pencil and the outline of the sides can be transferred to the ends of the braces.

Trim the length of the braces to clear the sides by 0.5mm/1⁄32" and refine the scalloping at the end of the braces so they are 3mm/1⁄8" high at the ends where they extend into the linings. Mark the position of the braces where they cross the linings and cut out a notch for the end of each brace. A sharp knife and a small chisel are the best tools, working slowly so not to spilt the linings or the sides. Check the fit so the back sits cleanly on the sides and linings.

Make sure the soundboard clamp that was fitted to hold the soundboard to the solera is removed before gluing on the back. There will be much regret if it is not. The simplest way to glue the back to the rest of the ukulele is with several large rubber bands. They can be looped through the slots in the workboard, or screws can be fixed around the edges of the workboard to act as anchoring points. Gluing the back while the rest of the instrument is flat on the workboard ensures that the soundboard and neck stay in the one plane. The importance of this will be seen when it comes to stringing up and playing the ukulele. The neck should be lightly clamped to the workboard and a couple of wooden cam-clamps can be used over the tailblock and heel. The back can be glued entirely with cam-clamps if enough are available.

TRIMMING AND BINDING

When the glue has dried the overhang of the soundboard and back can be trimmed flush with the sides. The safest way this can be done is with a sharp chisel although a small router and flush-trimming bit can be used with care on the thin and fragile soundboard and back. Clean up the edges with 80-grit sandpaper and a cork block and cut the rebate for

Gluing the fretboard with a plywood caul. Holes are drilled to clear the locating pins.

the binding if that is to be used. **Chapter 8** describes various styles of binding as well as ways to cut the binding rebate and glue the binding in place.

Leave the binding to dry overnight and then sand everything flush with 80- then 120-grit sandpaper. On the face of the soundboard continue sanding to 180-grit then 240-grit as the next step is gluing the fretboard, and it is easier not to have to do the final sanding on the soundboard with the fretboard in place.

GLUING THE FRETBOARD

A caul should be used for even clamping pressure over the entire fretboard. This is a piece of plywood 2mm/3⁄32" narrower than the fretboard itself with holes drilled to clear the locating pins. If a slight arch has been planed into the fretboard cross-section, the centre of the caul can be relieved a little or narrow strips of veneer glued along the edges of the caul.

Brush or blow any dust out of the locating pin holes on the top of the neck. Lightly sand the bottom of the fretboard to counter any oxidation and wipe with acetone to remove any residual oils. Insert the pins and apply glue to the fretboard, keeping it away from the edges where it extends over the soundboard to prevent squeeze-out onto the soundboard. This is one gluing procedure on the ukulele where epoxy is suggested. Water based glues, whether hot animal glue or modern aliphatic resins, will add moisture to the wood being glued. There is the chance of some swelling, bending the neck back and out of the flat plane required. At the same time, if the gluing is done in low humidity with a solid caul holding everything in place, the chance of warpage are minimal with water based glues. Epoxy is messier to use and there are people who have strong allergic reactions to it.

The locating pins will hold the fretboard in the correct position on the neck while the caul is fitted and clamps applied. Any glue squeeze-out along the sides of the neck itself can be left, as it can be sanded away later, but it must be removed from the nut slot and where the fretboard extends over the soundboard. This is why it was suggested to keep the glue well away from the edges! A plastic drinking straw cut at an angle works well for scooping most of it away. For water-based glues a piece of cloth and warm water is needed, but epoxy needs to be carefully removed with acetone.

Leave the glue to dry overnight (especially if epoxy is used). Remove the two locating pins, clean those slots of any excess glue and install the last two frets. Use a wooden block under the second fret to support the neck as the fret is hammered or pressed into place. Check the height of those two frets in relation to the others and file the ends flush with the edge of the fretboard.

THE FINAL STEPS

Trim the width of the neck to that of the fretboard if necessary, cleaning up any glue squeeze-out along the edges of the fretboard. The final shape of the neck shaft can now be carved. That is described in **Chapter 13**.

If a wipe-on finish is used, the bridge can be glued in place and the finish applied. **Chapter 15** deals with the options for finishing the ukulele. For a sprayed finish it is simpler to spray the entire soundboard and then remove the finish under where the bridge is to be glued. **Chapter 14** deals with the various styles of ukulele bridges.

CHAPTER 11
TENOR UKULELE

This chapter describes the assembly of the two tenor ukuleles, but this methodology can be used for any size of ukulele. The depth of the body mould would need to be adjusted to suit the size of the instrument.

A SEPARATE NECK

The early Hawaiian-made ukuleles used an integral neck construction, as shown in the 1917 film and described in **Chapter 12.** The Chicago and East Coast factories in the United States adapted guitar building techniques to ukuleles when mass production of the began in the mid-1910s. This included making the neck and body separately and bringing them together as one of the last stages of the building process. The usual neck attachment for American guitars was a tapered dovetail joint, which can be made accurately and repeatably with jigs and power driven cutters. It is a more complex woodworking task with hand tools with the neck having to be accurately positioned in three axes.

There are other ways the neck can be fixed to the body. At its simplest the neck heel need only butt up to the body and be glued in place. The low string tension of the smaller ukuleles does make this possible, but a more structural glue joint or mechanical fixing of some kind is better. The soprano ukulele (**Chapter 9**) uses a violin-style tapered mortice, which matches the taper of the neck heel and extends 6mm/¼" into the neck block.

A hardware alternative which has become popular in the past couple of decades in the guitar world is the 'bolt-on' neck. A metal insert is fitted to the neck heel and mates with a bolt through the neck block. The heel is usually made with a tenon which locates the neck in a mortice cut into the neck block. A barrel-nut can be fitted horizontally in the tenon or a threaded insert can be screwed into a pre-drilled hole. Guitar builders mostly use inserts with ¼" or M6 threads. These are relatively large and heavy, and not necessary for the smaller size of the ukulele.

The tenor ukulele uses an insert with an internal M4 thread. This is screwed into the tenon with 5-minute epoxy as a lubricant/adhesive. The size of the pilot hole will depend on the insert obtained, but it needs to be slightly larger than the maximum diameter of the shaft of the insert, but less than the diameter of the external cutting/locking threads.

The basics of neck construction are the same for a bolt-on neck as they are for a integral Spanish heel neck. The major difference is that the neck more or less ends where it joins the body and there is a solid wooden neckblock glued into the body that forms a attachment point for the soundboard, back and the sides, as well as the neck itself. The test fitting of the neck is done after the soundboard is glued to the sides and blocks, but before the back is glued in place.

The basic processes of neck construction are covered in **Chapter 6,** which covers the marking out of the neck profile on the neck blank and the shaping of the head. Assembly of the body and fitting the neck to the separate body are covered in this chapter.

THE SIDE ASSEMBLY

The soundboard and back should be constructed as directed in **Chapter 4** and the sides bent into shape as per **Chapter 5**. For this tenor ukulele the sides were shaped in the Fox Bender. They were made from mahogany 75mm/3" wide and 2mm/0.080" thick. Once the heat blanket was up to temperature the sides were pulled into shape and cooked for four minutes at 150°C/300°F. The temperature was reduced to 100°C/212°F and left for another 10 minutes. The

The bent linings drying in the Fox bending jig.

blanket was then turned off and the sides allowed to cool. Those temperatures are approximate and are from the markings on the controller supplied with the heat blanket.

Solid linings were also bent. These are made 8mm/5⁄16" wide and 2.5mm/3⁄32" thick. They can be cut from excess width of the sides or softwood. In this case side offcuts were used for the back linings and softwood offcuts for the soundboard linings. A double thickness was used for the soundboard edge and a single layer for the back.

The tenor tailblock is laminated from three pieces of spruce 5mm/3⁄16" thick. The outside pieces have the grain following that of the sides. The centre laminate has the grain at 90° to the outside layers so the endgrain is visible on the top and bottom of the block. The pieces are cut out a few mm oversize and the glued up block cut to 50mm/2" wide and 72mm/2⅞" high. Centrelines should be marked and one side is shaped to fit the curvature of the mould at the tail. **Chapter 5** describes the construction of the laminated tailblock.

The tenor neck block is a solid piece of mahogany or other mid-weight hardwood such as koa, walnut or Queensland maple. It is 62mm/2½" high, 50mm/2" wide and 25mm/1" thick. Again, one of the 50mm/2" wide faces is shaped to fit the curvature of the mould. The block should be oriented so the end-grain is on the sides of the block that nothing gets glued to. This means that the grain is going in the same direction as that of the sides and may be more susceptible to splitting. On the other hand there is no gluing to end-grain.

Cut the sides to length so they are seated firmly in the mould and the ends butt up evenly where the mould halves join. A strip of masking tape over the join on the outside will stop glue leakage though the join. This can otherwise adhere the sides to the mould itself when the blocks are glued and clamped in place. The mould should be placed on a flat surface (such as the workbench or auxiliary workboard) with the edges that will be glued to the soundboard pushed down to the flat surface. The sides should protrude 6-10mm/¼-⅜".

Smear glue on the curved faces of each block, locate the marked centrelines to the join of the mould halves and clamp them into position, ensuring that the bottom of each block is sitting on the supporting flat surface. The tail block can be held to the protruding sides by a couple of spring clamps if required.

Once the glue is dry remove the clamps and loosen the spreader blocks so the sides and block assembly can be pushed through the mould so the soundboard edge protrudes. Fit and glue the soundboard linings. In this case two thickness of solid linings were used, but kerfed linings are an alternative. The two layers of bindings can be glued at the one time, sitting above the sides by around 0.5mm/1⁄32". Adjust them as the spring clamps are attached to ensure the inside edges are lined up, as it looks neater.

Leave this overnight before removing the clamps and plane or sand the linings flush with the sides. Keep the side and block assembly firmly clamped by the spreader blocks to the mould. This will ensure the the finished side/lining surface is in the one plane. It is quite easy to sand a dip into the waist area if the side/ block assembly is allowed to flex when the levelling is done.

THE SIDE TAPER

The next procedure is to shape the bottom edges of the sides so the depth of the body tapers from the tailblock to the neck join. There are a couple of ways to approach this. One is to have a straight taper from tail to neck, with a transverse curve forced onto the back from one or two transverse back braces. A slight bevel needs to be sanded into the edge of the sides and the linings for a neat glue join to the back. This is an old Spanish guitar building methodology, now sadly out of fashion.

The modern approach is to use a concave sanding dish to shape the sides, the neck extension and the tail block into a section of a sphere. The section in **Chapter 3** on **Workboards** describes the construction of a concave sanding dish and the mounting of an axle in an auxiliary workboard.

The sides are only 1.5-2mm/0.060-0.080" thick and will cut easily with a sharp chisel or a block plane. At the same time they are fragile and care must be taken to prevent splitting along the grain.

On the outside, mark the desired finished height of the neck and tail blocks - 56mm/2¼" and 69mm/2¹¹⁄₁₆" for the tenor ukuleles. If the concave sanding dish is to be used, also mark the tail depth at the waist. The roughly circular shape of the lower bout means that the sides are close to the same depth from the tail to the waist, and then noticeably dip to the neck block.

Replace the side assembly back in the mould and push it through so the back edges of the sides protrude. The side assembly must protrude enough so the bottom of the neck block can be shaped to

Marking the lengths of a side in the mould so the two sides meet cleanly on the centreline at each end. Extra clamps may be used to pull the sides into the mould. The spreader blocks hold the sides firmly in place.

Above: The two sides trimmed to length and ready for the blocks to be glued in place.

Below: One large G-clamp is used to glue each block, with two spring clamps to glue the tailblock where it extends above the mould.

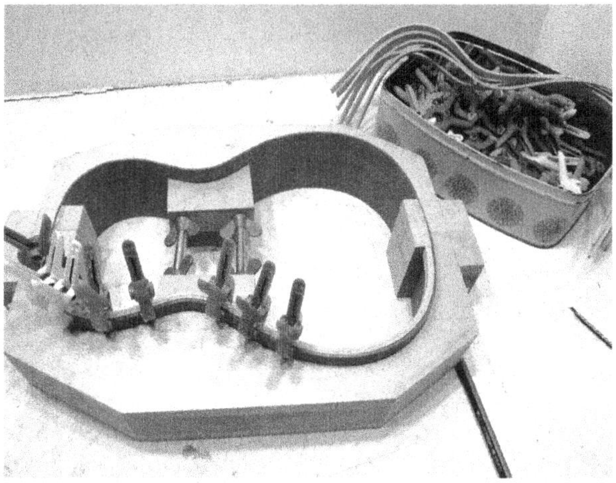

Holding the lining strip in place with a few spring clamps to mark the fit at the tailblock.

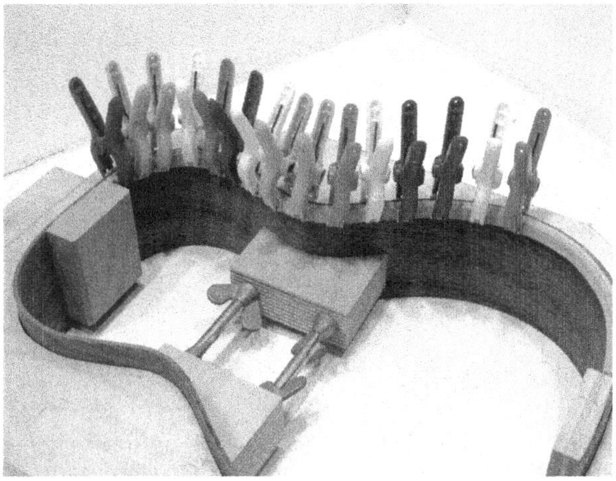

Above: Gluing two layers of linings on the soundboard edge.

Below: The soundboard linings glued and clamped.

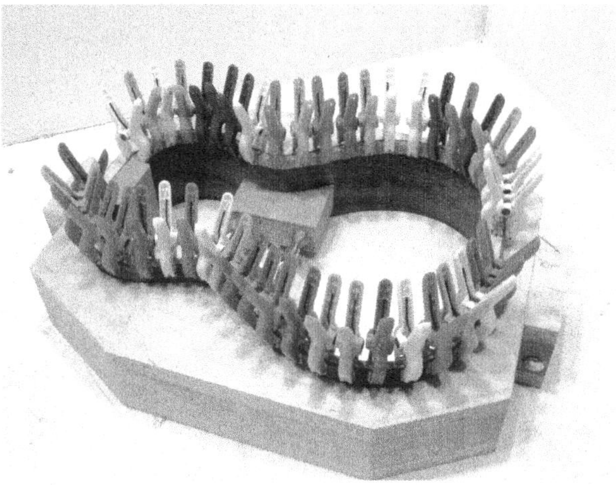

follow the body taper. It can be useful to use four small blocks of timber or plywood of the same thickness. These are placed inside the mould under the neck and tailbacks and the waist to ensure the sides are sitting square and evenly protruding. The spreader blocks can then clamp the sides firmly into the mould for shaping.

THE STRAIGHT TAPER

For the straight tapered back, chisel or plane the sides carefully, sighting down the body to check the line of the trimming and measure the depth of the sides at opposite points to ensure symmetry.

The back edge of the neck block will end up a couple of millimetres higher than the front (where it is glued to the sides) because of the body taper. A large flat sanding board, a piece of melamine-faced MDF the size of at least two sheets of sandpaper, is very useful to refine the entire plane of the back edge of the sides. A smaller sanding block can be used to sand the small bevel to account for the transverse curvature of the back induced by the braces.

THE DOMED BACK

The sanding dish works best when rotated around an axle, in this case a short length of 15mm/⅝″ metal curtain rod (which was what was available at the time). The solera workboards used to assemble the Spanish heel style of ukulele incorporate a hole for this axle, or a dedicated work board can be made from a piece of ply or MDF. The mould needs to be held firmly in position with the axle hole aligned with the centreline of the mould around the waist position. Vertical holes can be drilled through the mould so it may be bolted to the workboard. Alternatively the mould can be held with four or more cauls using ¼″ hanger bolts and wing-nuts that fit into slots cut into the workboard.

Care must be taken to sand the sides evenly. It is remarkably simple to sand one side noticeably lower than the other. Check regularly with a ruler at opposite points on the sides. Shape the sides and blocks almost to the pencil marks on the neck and tail block, ensuring that the top surfaces of the blocks are entirely covered with sanding marks. A line of chalk will show any low points as the sanding progresses.

The side assembly should be left in the mould while the back linings are fitted and glued with as many small spring clamps as can be fitted. Check that the spreader blocks can be loosened enough so they can be removed with the back linings installed. A single strip of solid linings 2.5mm/0.1" wide is sufficient or kerfed linings 5mm/3⁄16" wide can be used. Because of the varying depth of the sides the linings will protrude a little unevenly, but this will be evened out with the sanding dish once the glue has dried. A minimum protrusion of around 1mm/1⁄32" will allow the linings and sides both have the slight bevel to match the spherical section of the back.

The side assembly in the mould can be reattached to the base used previously, and the sanding dish used to sand down to the pencil marks at each end, being careful to maintain evenness on both sides. The assembly can be left in the mould for the fitting of the soundboard and back to ensure it stays in shape.

Place the soundboard on the bench with the side assembly on top. Line up the centrelines on both neck and tail blocks with the centreline marked on the inside of the soundboard. Use a pencil to mark on both where the linings meet the two transverse braces. Check that the height of the braces at that point is 3mm/1⁄8" and adjust that if necessary. Trim the length of the braces so they extend halfway into the linings and cut notches 3mm/1⁄8" deep in the linings to suit. There should be a gap of around 1mm/1⁄32" between the ends of the braces and the back of the notch. This gives a little adjustment room when gluing the soundboard to the sides. Make sure the notches are deep enough for the linings and blocks to sit evenly on the soundboard.

Repeat the process to fit the back and set the back aside until the neck is fitted.

If the neck is made with the 'tongue' extension under the fingerboard into the body, that slot should be cut into the soundboard before the soundboard is glued to the sides. The tongue is 18mm/3⁄4" wide, so a Forstner bit of that size is used to drill a hole on the centreline just above the upper transverse

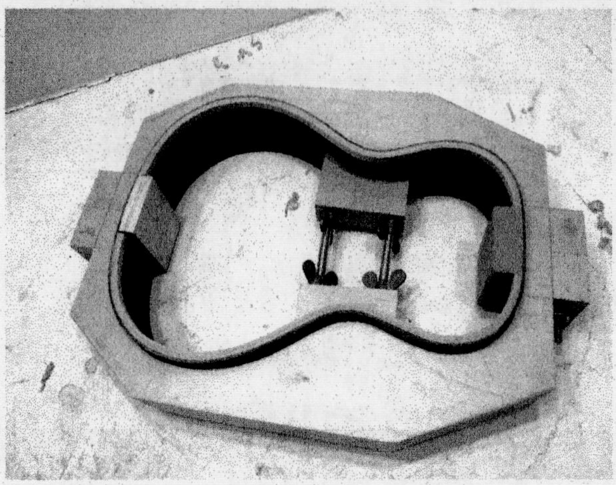

Soundboard linings trimmed flush with the sides.

Above: The curtain rod axle for the sanding dish. The blue chalk on the edges of the sides show any low points during the sanding process. The small plywood supports under the neck and tailblocks, as well as the waist can be be seen. A solera workboard is used as a base for the sanding dish axle.

Below: One side of the back linings glued in place.

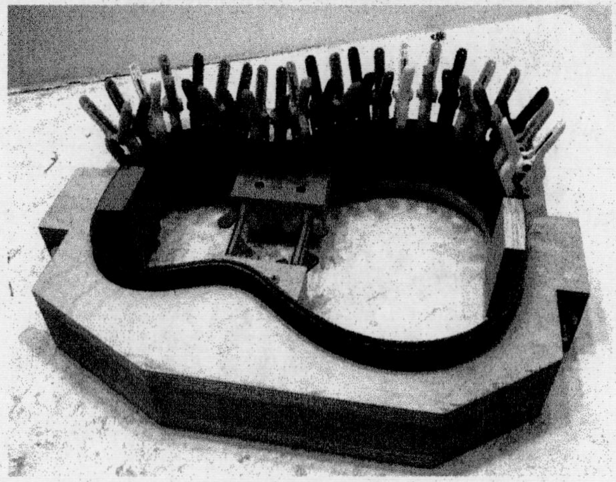

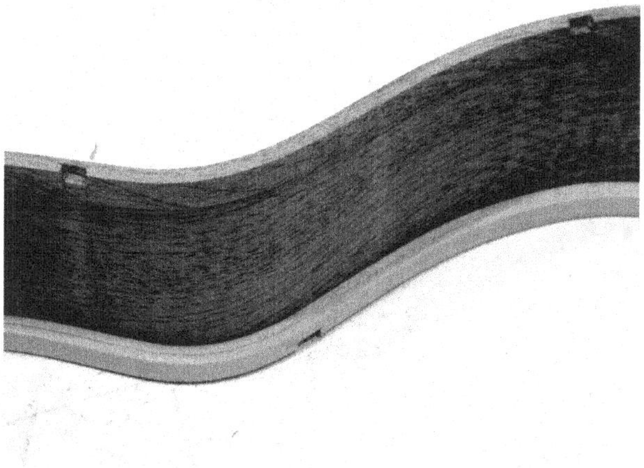

Notches cut into the soundboard and back linings to locate the back and soundboard braces.

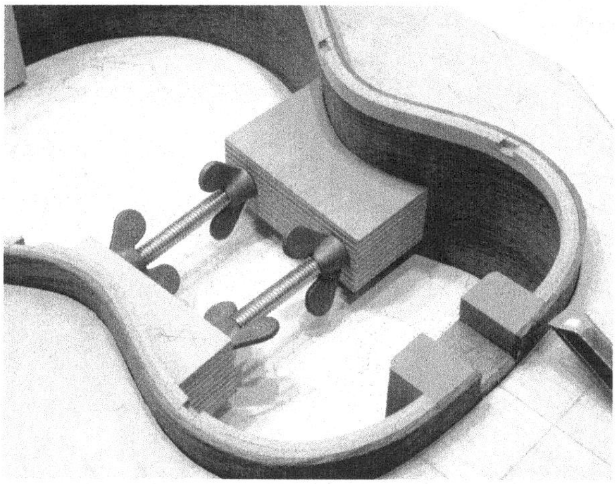

Above: The notches in the soundboard linings for the two transverse braces and the slot cut for the neck extension tongue.

brace, cutting halfway through from the top and then turned over and the remainder cut from the inside. This minimises the possibility of splintering. Knife cuts extend the slot back to the neck block and the waste removed. A photo on page 91 shows the slot cut into the soundboard.

The soundboard should now be glued to the sides using whatever kind of clamps are available. Run a thin line of glue around the linings and blocks and bring together. Clamp the neck and tail blocks first, taking care to keep them square to the soundboard. This is to ensure that the gluing surfaces meet as exactly as possible. Then add more clamps gently. Over-tightening the clamps can pull the sides out of square and not much clamping pressure is needed to hold the sides and linings to the flat soundboard. Any squeeze-out on the inside can be cleaned up with a damp cloth or paper towel. Once the glue is dry, trim back any overhang of the soundboard with a chisel or sanding block.

The side assembly could be left in the mould during the gluing of the soundboard if desired.

FITTING A BOLT-ON NECK

For a ukulele with a separate neck attached with a straight tenon the next step is to fit the back of the heel and the tenon to the end of the body so that:

Below: Test fitting the soundboard to the sides. The slot for the neck extension tongue has not yet been cut into the soundboard.

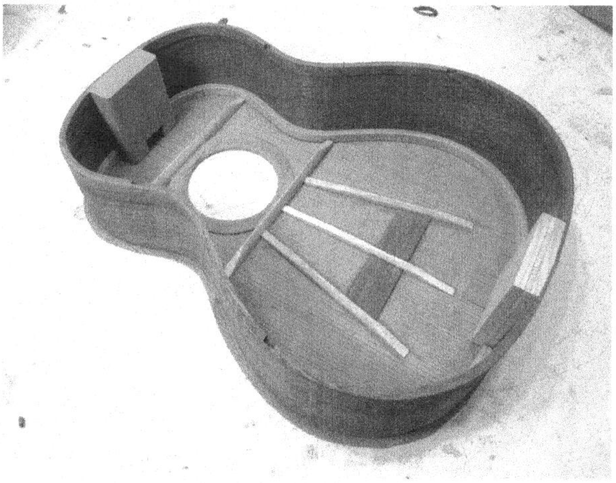

Below: The soundboard being glued to the sides. Light clamping pressure is used to keep the sides vertical to the soundboard.

1 - there is no gap between the heel and the sides,
2 - the centrelines of both the body and the neck line up,
3 - the top of the neck and the soundboard are in the same plane.

This can be done with a chisel and sanding sticks: small lengths of timber 12 x 6mm/½ x ¼" with 80-grit sandpaper glued to one or more sides.

It is easier if the back surface and edges of the heel and the tenon are shaped to final dimensions before the rest of the neck. It is important that the centrelines of both the neck and body are aligned. This might involve trimming material from one side or the other of the heel. It is a convention that the fret at which the neck joins the body (usually the 12th or 14th) lines up with the body edges. If the back of the heel has to be trimmed to line up the centrelines, it might put a pre-determined nut position a little further up the neck than is preferable. It can be an advantage not to have finalised the break point of the head and nut before the heel is fully trimmed to shape. It should only ever be a shift of a millimetre or two but it can help the look of the finished instrument to get the distance from the body join to the front of the nut just right.

The 12 fret tenor neck also includes a shallow extension of the neck into the body under the fretboard. This 'tongue' is the same 18mm/¾" width of the tenon and also assists with the alignment of the neck. This is optional as the fretboard over the body can simply be glued lightly to the soundboard instead of being supported by the tongue. The 14 fret tenor ukulele uses this approach.

The top surface of the neck has to be in the same plane as the soundboard. This happens automatically when using a solera workboard, but not necessarily when using a bolt-on neck. A sliding bevel is used to check the angle between the soundboard surface and

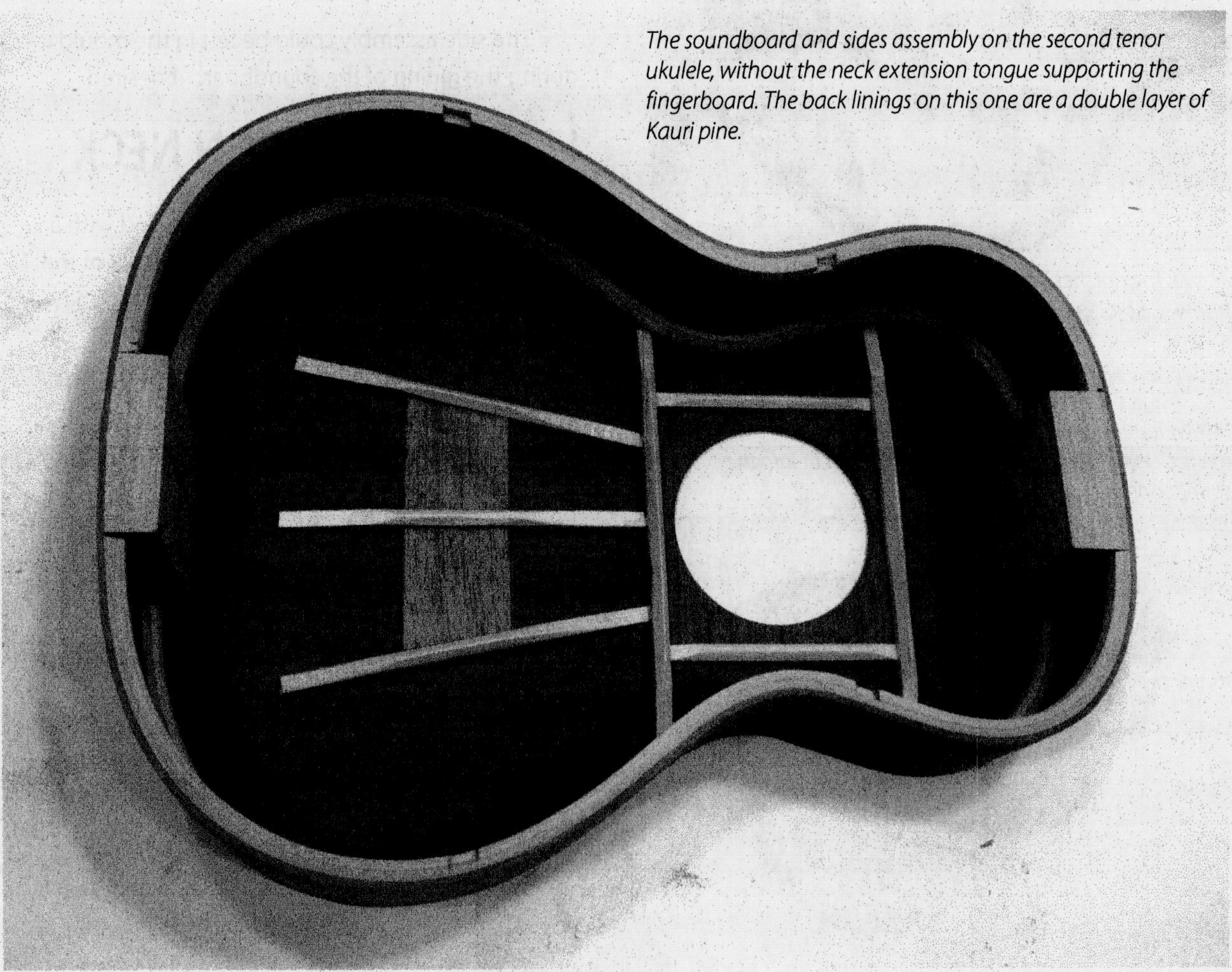

The soundboard and sides assembly on the second tenor ukulele, without the neck extension tongue supporting the fingerboard. The back linings on this one are a double layer of Kauri pine.

The tenor ukulele soundboard cut out for the extension tongue.

Cutting the body mortice for the bolt-on tenor neck.

Below: Clamping the small support braces on either side of the cut-out in the soundboard.

the end of the body. That angle, if any, is transferred to the sides of the heel at the 12th fret position and a saw cut made to 10mm/3⁄8″ from the centreline. This has to be cut as accurately and cleanly as possible and a good handsaw can be safer than a bandsaw. The tenon and the tongue extension are 10mm/3⁄8″ deep and the excess can be trimmed off with a band or handsaw and cleaned up with a chisel. The tongue should extend to 1.5mm/1⁄16″ before the upper transverse brace and the end shaped to a semi-circle to match the slot cut into the soundboard.

A matching mortice 12mm/½″ deep is cut into the neck block on the bandsaw with the soundboard face down on the saw table. This should ensure the sides of the mortice are vertical to the soundboard. The mortice should be cut a little undersized and the width extended with a chisel to match the tenon.

Drill a hole, to match the neck attachment bolt used, through the centre of the neck block. The tenor neck block is 56mm/2¼″ high and the hole is drilled 40mm/19⁄16″ from the top (or 16mm/5⁄8″ from the bottom).

A small saw and a chisel is used to cut a horizontal section 10mm/3⁄8″ deep from the top of the neck block to accept the tongue extension. The previous cut slot in the soundboard will guide the width. The edges of the soundboard slot are reenforced on the inside by small (6mm/¼″ square) braces glued on either side between the neck block and the upper transverse brace.

Before the neck can be finally fitted to the body, the heel must be trimmed to the width of the fretboard at the body join. For a 12th fret body join this is 45mm/1¾″ and the heel can be kept at that width if desired rather than tapering towards the back.

If the heel is to be tapered care must be taken to allow for the slight curvature of the sides as they curve into the meeting point at the end of the body. The back of the heel on either side of the mortise can be slightly undercut, leaving a 3mm/1⁄8″ wide contact strip more easily adjusted to allow for the curves of the sides.

The width of the neck can be cut to within a millimetre or so of the fretboard and trimmed to the fretboard width with a chisel. The final width of the heel is marked on the inside and also trimmed with a chisel. The fretboard clamped to the neck acts as a guide for this trimming.

The fretboard can be removed and the neck checked for fit. The tenon and the extension tongue should slide into the mortice, but the sides of the heel will stop a short distance from the body as no allowance has been made yet for the curvature at the end of the body. Mark a strip 3mm/⅛" wide on the edges of the back of the heel and undercut inside those marks towards the tenon. This will make the tenon slightly longer and the outside of the heel will eventually just touch the sides.

Check the alignment of the centrelines and adjust by trimming where the edges of the heel meet the body if necessary. Also check that the top surface of the neck is in line with the top of the neck, both longitudinally and laterally. Once the neck is correctly fitted hold it firmly in place and mark the position of the threaded neck insert using the bit used to drill the bolt mounting hole from the inside.

The M4 thread insert used are 10mm/⅜" long and require a 6mm/¼" pilot hole a little longer than the insert. Check the size of the insert before drilling as they do vary. Too small a pilot hole could lead to the heel splitting and too large a hole might mean insufficient grip for the external threads. The pilot hole can be carefully hand-drilled, keeping it as close as possible to aligned centrally. The wood threads of the insert are smeared with 5-minute epoxy and it is screwed in with a matching Allen key.

Holding the neck in place to the body, test fit the bolt into the insert and tighten. Check the alignment of the centrelines and the plane of top of the neck and the soundboard. Adjust as necessary until everything lines up.

Remove the neck and glue the back in place. The back braces should fit neatly into the notches cut into the back linings. Two methods of clamping the back

Sawing the back of the heel to match the angle between the end of the body and the soundboard. This ensures the top of the neck is in the same plane as the soundboard.

Above: Bandsawing the thickness of the extension tongue.

Below: Bandsawing the width of the tongue.

Above: Fitting the threaded insert with an Allen key.

An M4 bolt holding the neck in position. The small braces on either side of the tongue can be seen.

Below: The insert and bolt fitted in the second tenor neck. On this one there is no extension tongue and it has a tapered heel.

in place have been used for these ukuleles. The first uses a ukulele shaped workboard with slots or wood screws around the edge. Large rubber bands can be used to apply clamping pressure. The second method uses a couple of wooden cam clamps for the blocks and shop-made spool clamps around the perimeter.

Once dry, trim the overhang and fit the binding and purfling, if used, as described in **Chapter 8**.

The first tenor ukulele used tortoise celluloid binding with a strip of 1mm/0.040″ black/white purfling the same depth as the binding. The white face of the purfling lightens the effect of the tortoise coloured celluloid. The bindings themselves are 1.5mm/0.060″ wide so a 2.5mm/0.100″ wide rebate must be cut around the edge to fit the bindings and purfling strip. The rebate is cut 4mm/0.160″ deep.

The plastic binding and the purfling are flexible enough that they can be glued and held in place with masking tape. Wood glue is used between the purfling and the soundboard/linings and solvent cement between the purfling and the binding. The second tenor ukulele with 14 frets to the body used rope binding, the manufacture and installation of which is also covered in **Chapter 8**.

The body can now be sanded to at least 180-grit and 240-grit on a softwood soundboard.

GLUING THE FRETBOARD

The fretboard, with all but two frets installed, should now be glued to the neck, either with epoxy or wood glue. A caul should be made from 12mm/½″ plywood with holes drilled to clear the two locating nails. The caul should be a millimetre or two slightly narrower than the fretboard itself. A strip of 3mm/⅛″ wide veneer should be glued along each edge to add more clamping pressure to the edges of the fretboard, especially if a slight arch was sanded across the board.

It can be useful to sand the neck surface lightly with a half-sheet sanding board to remove any surface oxidation of the wood before brushing or blowing any dust clear. Wipe down the underneath surface of the fretboard itself with acetone to ensure it is clean of any oils. This is important if a rosewood fingerboard is used.

Apply the glue, fit the nails through the fret slots and into the neck and clamp in place with the caul. Carefully clean up any squeeze-out around the back of the heel and the extension tongue as any dollops of dried glue will interfere with the neck fit. Similarly clean the nut slot of any squeeze-out. Leave to dry overnight before removing the clamps, cleaning out the two empty fret slots and installing the last two frets. Trim the width of the neck to that of the fretboard, cleaning up any glue squeeze-out along the edges of the fretboard. The final shape of the neck shaft can now be carved. That is described in **Chapter 13**.

If a sprayed finish is to be applied, the body and the neck can be finished separately before re-attaching the neck and subsequently gluing the bridge in place. For a wipe-on finish the neck can be re-attached at this stage. If the simpler mortice was used, the fretboard should be lightly glued (just a drop towards the end) to the soundboard to stop any vibration. The bridge can be glued in place and the finish applied. **Chapter 16** deals with the options for finishing the ukulele.

The back of a tenor ukulele glued in place with rubber bands.

The back of the other tenor ukulele being glued in place with a mix of spool and wooden cam clamps.

Below: The fretboard glued with a caul. The clearance hole for the locating pin at the second fret slot can be seen.

Below: The fretboard glued to the neck and onto the supporting tongue.

CHAPTER 9
AN OLD ISLAND STYLE SOPRANO

The original Hawaiian instruments had smaller and more tightly waisted bodies than later instruments. C.F. Martin & Co introduced a line of ukuleles in 1916 that used a slightly larger and rounder shape that is still a standard and the Chicago factories made similar, if not as refined, instruments by the tens of thousands.

This soprano ukulele follows (more or less) an older methodology that was depicted in a short film produced by the Ford Motor Company in 1917. The person assembling the instrument was probably an employee of Manuel Nunes (who appears briefly) and the film shows a now almost forgotten approach to ukulele construction. It uses an inside mould sitting on a T base. The longer arm of the T holds the neck with a Spanish heel style of integral neck block, while the cross pieces support shaped cauls which are wedged to clamp the sides to the mould at the waist.

The neck is held in position by rope and more wedges while the sides are fitted into the neck block slots and the waist cauls wedged into place. The film does not show the fitting or gluing of the sides to the tail block, but that is achieved in some way, perhaps again using rope or a single clamp and a shaped caul. The back linings and a single arched back brace are fitted before the back is glued and held on with more rope. At this point it is removed from the mould and the soundboard linings and two transverse braces are fitted. A large caul is then used to clamp the soundboard in place, probably with more rope as well as a G-clamp on the neck. This ensures that the neck and soundboard are kept in the same plane. The frets are inserted into slots cut into the neck itself before a bridge is fitted and the instrument polished.

There is a lot not shown in the film, such as the preparation of the thin pieces of wood used for the sides, the cutting of the fret slots and attaching the bridge. The film is less than three and a half minutes long, but there is enough information there to use as a basis for making a simple ukulele in what we might call an *Old Island Style*, though the methodology is probably as much Madieran as Hawaiian.

This design of this ukulele is based on an article written by a Los Angeles 'manual arts' teacher, John Bangerter, and originally published in the December 1915 edition of *The Industrial Arts Magazine*. The article included the plan of a ukulele and this instrument is a combination of the Ford company's film and Bangerter's article and plan. Ukulele historian John King republished it on his *Nalu Music* website, noting Bangerter's rather fanciful ideas about fret placement.

Many thanks to ukulele maker Ken Timms for his inspirational interpretation of the Ford film.

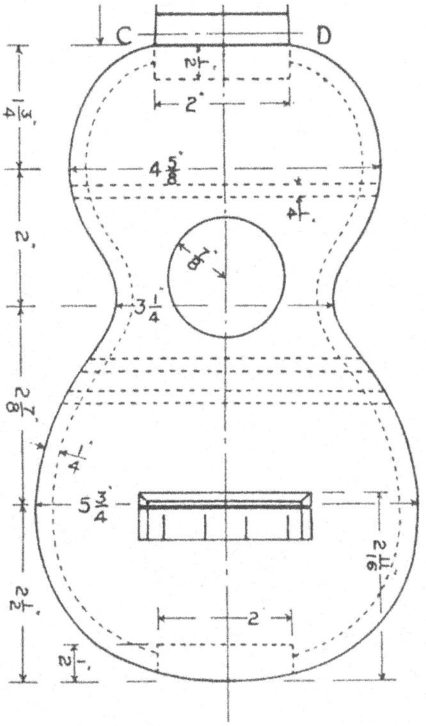

MAKING THE MOULD

The mould can be made from whatever stable materials there are on hand. The inside form itself has been made from two pieces of 18mm/3/4" marine ply cut out 1.5mm/.060" smaller than the outside plan of the instrument. A card template can be cut out 1.5mm/.060" smaller than the outside shape, which will also be useful when shaping the tailblock. The neck support and cross-piece are from a piece of scrap hardwood. The neck support was machined to 50mm wide, as this is the maximum width of the neck and the cross pieces to 30mm/1³⁄₁₆". The inside form was shimmed 1.5mm/.060" above the lengthwise neck support so that when the sides are fitted into the slots in the neck, they can be lined up with the bottom of the inside form, and leave space for the soundboard to be attached in the same plane as the neck. The thickness of the inside form has been trimmed 6mm/.25" towards the neck to allow for the body taper and the linings to be glued into place. The waist cauls are offcuts from the cutting out of the inside form and shaped to allow for the 1.5mm/.060" thickness of the sides.

Gluing the soundboard shim to the mould base.

The finished mould with the waist cauls and wedges.

Below: Cutting out the inside mould.

Below: With the waist cauls wedged into place.

THE NECK

This style of construction requires that the neck be mostly complete before the rest of the construction. The simplest approach is to cut the neck profile from a dressed 50mm/2″ square quarter-sawn block of timber 35cm/14″ long. The widest section of the fingerboard, where it meets the body is 50mm/2″ wide and the depth of the body at the neck join is 45mm/1¾″, so the 50mm/2″ is the minimum width. If the block is a little wider that will allow more flexibility in the shape (or at least width) of the head, but that is not essential.

As the 12th fret gets placed right on the line where the neck joins the soundboard, the slots cut into the neck to accept the sides must be straight and at right angles to the centreline. (On a classical guitar these slots are angled by a degree or two to follow the curve of the upper bout.) The slots need to be 1.5mm/.060″ wide with the front of the slot on the line of the 12th fret. Cut the slots (with whatever kind of saw you want) to within 3mm/⅛″ of the centreline of the top surface of the neck.

Cutting the fret slots into the top surface of the neck. The saw is fitted with an adjustable stop for consistent depth of the fret slots.

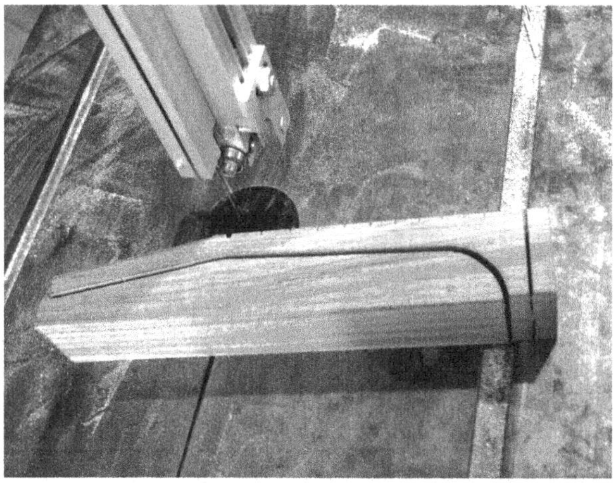

The neck profile sawn after the side and fret slots have been already cut.

Any of the other neck construction methods as outlined in **Chapter 6** can be used if a suitable 50mm/2″ square piece of wood cannot be obtained.

As the frets are to be inserted directly into the neck itself, it makes sense to cut the fret slots while the neck is still a square block. The 12th fret is placed where the neck joins the soundboard and there needs to be 13mm/½″ of neck extending into the body. The suggested 35cm/14″ length of the block allows a bit extra at either end, so mark the 12th fret position 25mm/1″ from the end of the block and the rest along the length of the block, adding another 3mm/⅛″ past the 0 fret so a slot can be chiseled out for a nut. Cut the slots 3mm/⅛″ deep. Sand the top surface to 180-grit and mark a centreline with a pencil.

The rest of the neck profile can then be cut out. On the side of the block mark a 14° line from the back of the nut slot the length of the head required, usually 100-110mm/ 4-4½″. The head should be 10mm/⅜″ thick at the end gradually getting a little thicker towards the nut. The neck should be 13mm/½″ thick just in front of the nut and 18mm/¾″ thick between the 8th and 9th frets. From that point it curves down to the heel. Cut the block to 45mm/1¾″ down from the fretboard surface at the heel, which should extend 10mm/⅜″ in front of the slots cut for the sides. There should also be 13mm/½″ of block extending into the body behind the slots. Cut this off square and sand the end-grain smooth. It can be worthwhile sealing the end-grain with shellac.

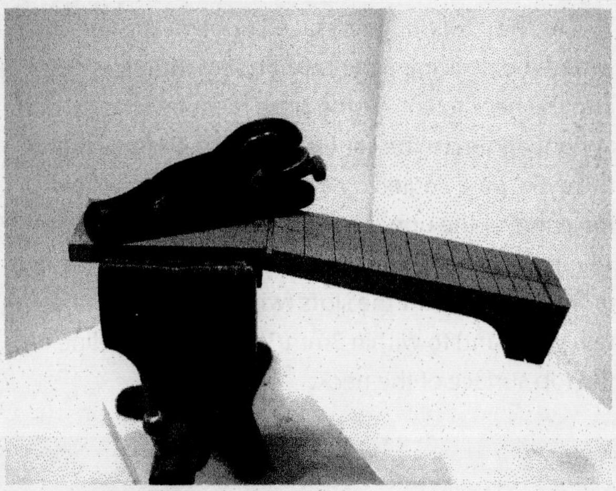

Planing the top surface of the head.

Plane the top surface of the head smooth and down to the marked line. A ledge the thickness of the soundboard (1.5mm/.060″) needs to be cut away from the top of the neck where it extends into the body. The top of the neck and the outside of the soundboard need to be in the same plane. This was the reason for the spacer between the base and the inside form of the mould.

Chiseling the soundboard ledge, which is the same depth as the shim on the base of the mould and the thickness of the soundboard.

The neck can now be tapered toward the nut, which is 35mm/1⅜″ wide, and the shape of the head cut out. This is most easily done on a bandsaw with the fretboard surface face down on the saw table and the trim lines marked on the back of the neck. Cut 1mm/1⁄32″ or so outside the line to allow for final shaping.

Mark and drill pilot holes for the tuners, again with the bottom surface of the head facing down on the drill-press so the holes are vertical in relation to that surface. The head tapers in thickness and if geared tuners are used it is better if the holes are perpendicular to where they are mounted.

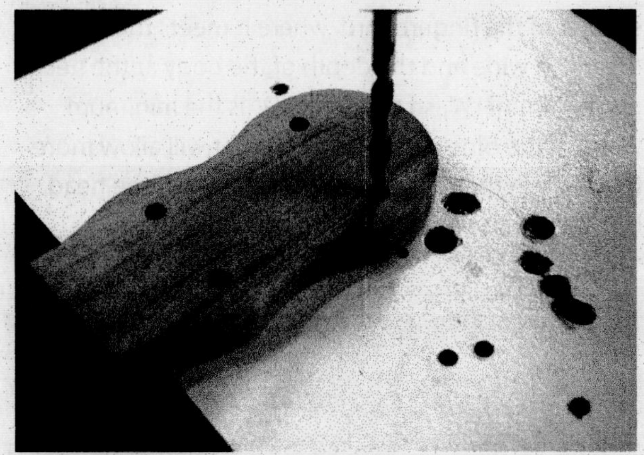

Drilling pilot holes for the tuners. If violin style tuners are used the hole should be slightly larger than the minimum diameter of the reamer.

Using a chisel refine the shape of the neck from the 12th fret to the nut. Continue the line of the neck into the flare of the head shape and finish shaping the head outline.

The heel needs to taper from 50mm/2″ wide on the top surface to 10mm/⅜″ wide where it meets the back, leaving the neck extension its original size to add gluing area when attaching the back. Start the heel taper from the bottom of the fret slots. Once the basic heel taper is carved, the shaping of the neck shaft can begin, starting the cross-section curve of the neck from the bottom of the fret slots.

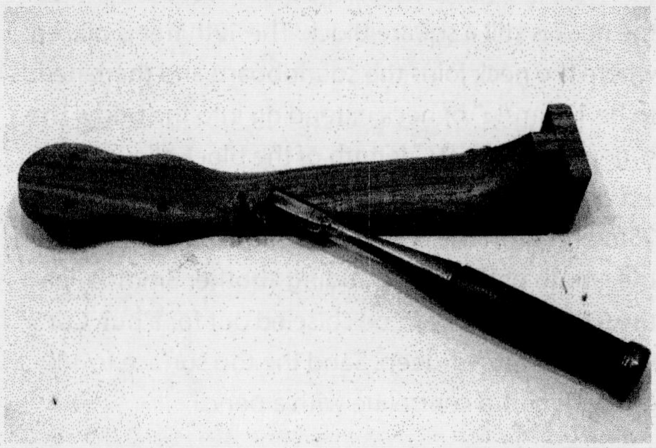

Carving the neck shaft.

The circles mark where the neck extension should be slightly relieved so the sides can fit more neatly (see text below).

The back of the finished neck.

Carve away the front of the neck block extension as it gets revealed by the heel taper. Even though the sides need to be straight as they fit into the neck slots, if the bottom corners of the neck block are relieved by 1.5mm/1⁄16" or so, it makes a more attractive curve of the back as it reaches the neck. The bent sides should happily fit to the curve while being forced straight at the soundboard edge. The circles in the photo above indicate the point of maximum relief on the neck block.

Below: The neck ready for assembly. The figure-of-eight shape for the head was commonly used on some of the early Hawaiian made instruments.

The neck is a series of continuously changing curves from the heel to the flat back of the head. The neck can be held in a bench vice or mounted on a cradle that supports the head and along the centreline. The shaping can be done with any combination of chisels, rasps, micro-planes or powered sanding drums. The important thing is that it feels comfortable in the hand when playing and the curves flow into each other when looked at from any angle. Sand to 180-grit.

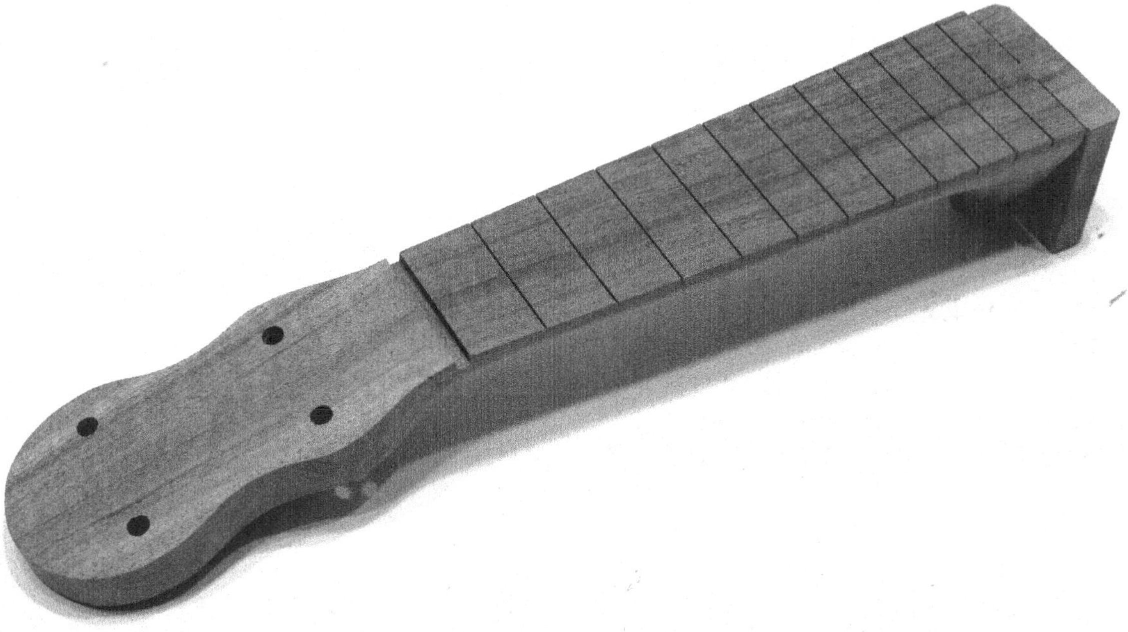

THE TAILBLOCK

A solid or laminated tailblock (See **Chapter 5**) 50mm/2″ wide, 53mm/2⅛″ high (a little longer than the sides are wide to allow trimming) and 13mm/½″ thick should be made. The outside should be shaped to match the curve of the sides at the tail.

THE SIDES

The sides on this little soprano need to be 35cm/14″ long, 50mm/2″ wide and 1.5mm/.060″thick. It is best to allow another 25mm/1″ at each end to make the bending easier. The sides can be bent to shape by any of the methods discussed in **Chapter 5**, keeping an overall 50mm/2″ width. Consider the grain patterns of the two halves and arrange the bending so where the sides meet at the tail the grain is closest to a mirror image or book-match. Also remember that as the sides enter the neck slots that will be straight on the soundboard edge and curved slightly at the back edge.

Attach the neck to the base of the mould. In the 1917 film, this is done by lashing the neck to the mould with rope and tightening that with one or more wooden wedges tapped in underneath. The two slots for the sides should line up to the edges of the inside form. Trim the neck ends of the sides so there is 22mm/⅞″ of *almost flat* section that will be inserted into the slots in the neck. The curve of the sides should start immediately outside the neckblock extension and follow the curves of the form closely. Do not worry if the rest of the curves are a little out of shape. The waist cauls and wedges will pull the sides into closer contact with the form, but the initial curve from the neck is important.

The neck lashed to the mould base, the sides held in place by the waist cauls and the tailblock clamped to the sides.

The length of the sides need to be trimmed so they meet exactly on the centreline of the tailblock, while following the curves of the inside form as closely as possible. The ends should be exactly square to the soundboard edges of the sides. It is better to have the sides a little short rather than too long, and bulge out from the form. A small gap at the tailblock can easily be filled later by an offcut from the soundboard or back, but it does look good to have a tight join at the tail.

If there is a high degree of confidence that the sides are the right length, the tailblock can be glued to the sides, off the form, and then returned to the form for gluing the sides into the neck slots.

GLUING THE NECK AND SIDES

The methodology illustrated in the film for this step is simple and direct. Glue is applied to slots in the neck and the sides inserted. The waist cauls and wedges are fitted and, in some way that is not shown in the film, the sides are glued and clamped to the tailblock. The obvious way to do this is with a clamp and the shaped caul mentioned above. The important thing to remember is to line up the soundboard edge of the sides with the lower edge of the inside form, leaving the sides the thickness of the soundboard (1.5mm/0.060″) above the top surface of the neck (where the frets will be inserted).

This is another of the those procedures where it is useful to go though the processes a couple of times without glue to feel how it all goes together.

TAPERING THE SIDES AND FITTING THE KERFED LININGS

The sides need to taper from 50mm at the tail to 45mm at the neck heel. The modern way to do this is with a concave sanding dish lined with coarse grit sandpaper. These would be typically shaped to a 4.6m/15′ radius and the back braces shaped to suit. The backs of the larger tenor and baritone ukuleles are done this way, but on this very small soprano instrument the simpler old Spanish method works fine. This involves simply shaping the sides with a small plane or chisel so when viewed from the side there is a straight line from the tail to the neck heel. A half sheet sanding block covered with 80-grit paper is useful for the final touches. The important thing to keep in mind is maintaining equal height on both sides. Check at the waist and the widest points of both the upper and lower bouts.

The linings are lengths of softwood 7mm x 5mm/ 9⁄32″ x 3⁄16″ with slots cut into the wider edge to allow the strip to be bent around the curves of the sides in the mould. The slots can be cut with a simple fixture which is piece of 16mm/5⁄8″ MDF the width of the bandsaw table with a slot cut which is a little less than the depth of the blade. This is clamped at each end to the bandsaw table with the blade protruding enough for a 4-4.5mm/5⁄32″ cut in the strips, leaving a 0.5-1mm/1⁄32″ flexible web on one side. The bandsaw blade will want to move back and forth a little as the strip is fed in for one cut at a time, so it may take a

Tapering the sides with a small plane.

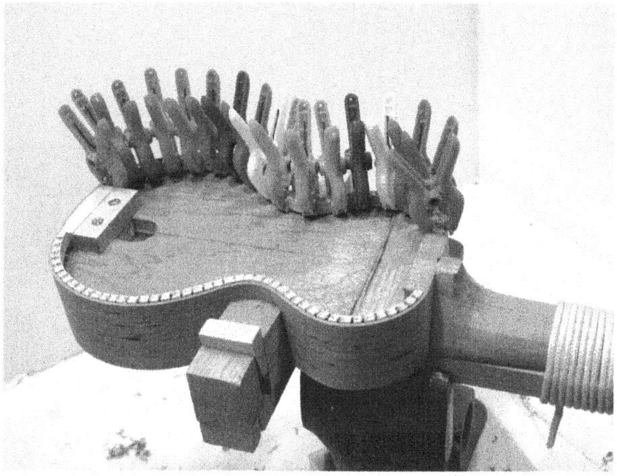

Gluing the kerfed lining for the back.

Below: Using a half-sheet sanding board to refine the sides as well as the neck and tail blocks.

Below: Leveling the back linings.

little tweaking of the position of the MDF for the best results. The slots should be cut 6mm/¼" apart, and a pencil mark to one side of the blade will assist with regularity. There is a photo of the jig in **Chapter 5.**

A 30cm/12" length will be adequate for each side, so four are required. They should be flexible enough to be bent into shape around the inside of each side and fitted neatly between the neck extension and the tailblock. It should be possible to bend the lining strips without breaking at all, but they might well want to crack a little at each cut point. This is perfectly OK and will help keep the bent shape while gluing. Smear the face of each strip which is opposite the webbing with glue and clamp into place with clothes-pegs or very small spring clamps. They should be glued in place with .5mm/1⁄32" or so above the edge for later trimming. With the webbing on the inside of the body, rather than being glued to the side, this is known as "reverse-kerf lining".

Once the glue is dry, plane, chisel or sand the linings down to just above the level of the sides.

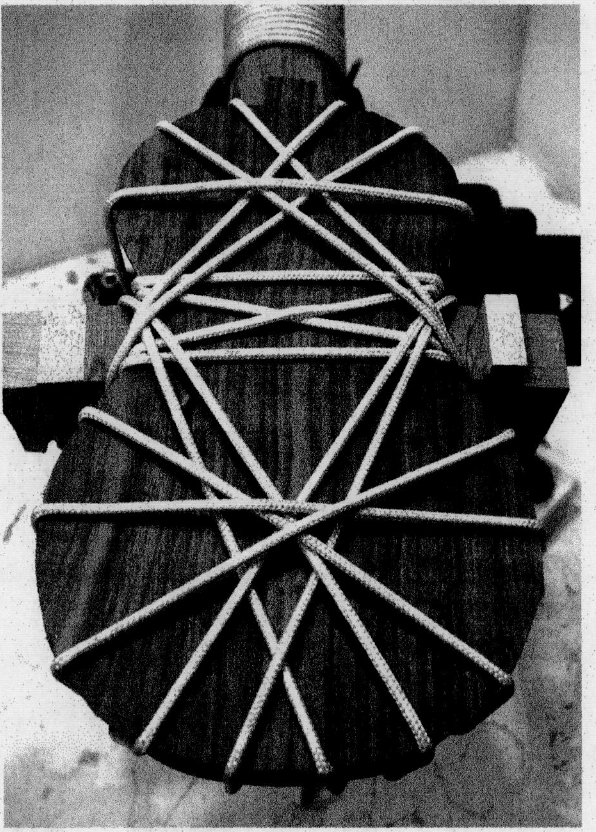

The back roped into place while the glue dries.

THE BACK BRACE AND GLUING THE BACK

The back on these instruments was almost always a single piece of koa around 1.5mm/0.060" thick, although some were a little thicker. They use only a single brace, 5mm/3⁄16" wide, on the back fitted around halfway along the body length, a little below the waist. This is notched into the linings and glued into place before the back is glued on. It should sit 4mm/5⁄32" into the linings and this one has 3mm/⅛" of rise to the middle, so the brace will have a total height of 7mm/9⁄32". Once the glue has dried, sand the slightly protruding linings and the sides to the slight bevel of the arch of the brace. This will make a cleaner join when the back is glued.

In the film the back is glued by wrapping the back and the entire mould with rope. This is an efficient and low-tech method of applying even gluing pressure, but it does need practice before doing it with glue. Up to 7-8m/25' of rope can be used and it has to be wrapped around evenly to ensure enough pressure especially at the neck, tailblock, the waist/brace and over the transverse brace.

The back needs to be only a millimetre or so larger than the outline of the sides. The thin timber can be easily split by the pressure of the rope if the overhang at the widest parts of the upper and lower bouts is any more than this.

THE SOUNDBOARD BRACING

Once the glue is dry after gluing the back, the assembly may be lifted from the mould. It should just slide off, once the rope holding the neck is removed. If necessary trim the tailblock to the height of the sides and repeat the process of installing the linings, again leaving them just a little above (.5mm/1⁄32") of the top edges of the sides. Sand the linings level and prepare two braces 5 x 10mm/3⁄16" x 3⁄8" from spruce or the same hardwood as the soundboard. Like the brace on the back, these two braces are glued into notches in the linings and the soundboard glued on afterwards. The ends of these two braces need to be scalloped so the ends are 3mm/1⁄8" high and can be supported by the linings. The face to which the soundboard will be glued is flat, without the arching of the back brace. The half-sheet sanding block can be used to level the linings, braces and tailblock.

THE SOUNDBOARD

Like the back, the soundboard was usually a single piece of timber. The simplest early ukuleles had no soundhole rosette or edge bindings, so all that is necessary is to cut a 22mm/7⁄8" radius soundhole at the appropriate spot once the wood has been thicknessed to 1.5mm/0.060". If a rosette is to be used, this is best inlaid while the soundboard is 3-4mm/0.120"-0.160" thick and the final thicknessing completed afterwards. The rosette can then be inlaid

The neck, sides and back assembly removed from the mould, showing the position of the back brace.

while around 1.5mm/0.060" thick with a final depth of around 0.75-1mm/0.030-0.040" into the soundboard. This maintains enough wood behind or below the rosette for structural integrity.

The rosette can be simple strips of purfling that contrast with the soundboard timber, such as maple for a koa soundboard. 2mm x 0.5mm/0.080 x 0.020" purfling strips are available from lutherie supply houses, as well as 0.7mm/0.028" thick sheets of veneer in various colours from which strips can be cut.

There are various ways the rosette grooves can be cut in the soundboard. A Dremel (or similar) miniature router with a small downcut bit in a jig which cuts a circular slot is one method. Both Stewart-MacDonald and Luthiers Mercantile sell bases for the Dremel, although they may need modification for the small radius circles used on ukuleles. Small, albeit fragile, spiral downcut bits are available in sizes from 0.5mm/0.020" up. Alternatively a simple device could be made with a small blade set into a block of wood that pivots on an old drill bit, and cuts a single pre-determined radius circle the depth of which is set by the projection of the blade. There are also several commercial versions of this tool available.

A simple rope-binding rosette.

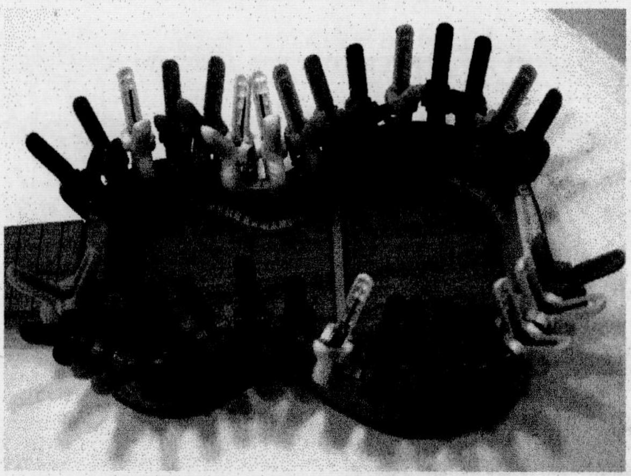

Gluing the soundboard linings.

Below: The soundboard braces glued into their notches.

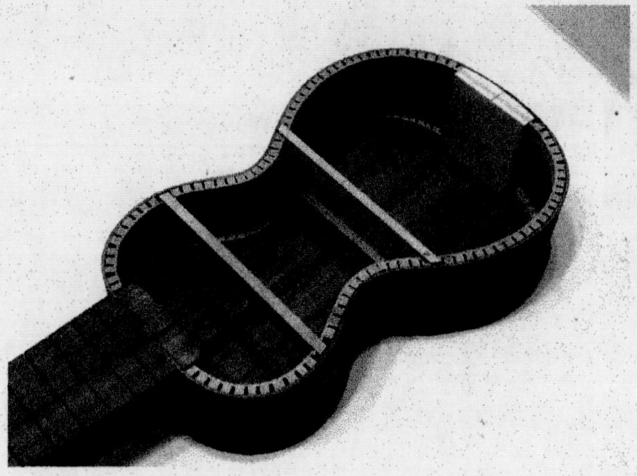

The better quality early Hawaiian ukuleles would often have a rosette made of a strip of rope binding matching that used around the soundboard edges, with a thin strip of purfling inside and out, separated by a couple of mm. **Chapter 4** details the construction of a rope rosette.

The soundboard in the Ford film is cut close to the body size with two small wings that fit either side of the neck to locate that end of the soundboard. The join of the sides at the tail should be on the centreline of the neck and body and this can be used to position that end of the soundboard for gluing. Care should be taken that the soundhole is centred on the waist and a pencil mark made where the soundboard will meet the tail join.

GLUING THE SOUNDBOARD

The Ford film uses a large and rigid flat caul that is the shape of the body and neck to align and clamp the soundboard to the rest of the ukulele. The one illustrated is made of two pieces of scrap 18mm/¾" melamine faced MDF screwed together. The neck top surface and the soundboard need to be in the same plane, so after glue is spread on the blocks, linings and braces, the soundboard is placed in position, the caul placed on top and clamped to the neck shaft. Add another clamp over the tailblock and wrap the body and caul with rope starting from the waist to ensure there is clamping pressure on the two soundboard braces.

Once dry the overhang of the soundboard can be trimmed off with a chisel and sanded smooth.

A soundboard with no rosette ready to be glued to the body.

BINDING (OPTIONAL)

If a rosette was inlaid around the soundhole, matching binding was commonly installed. **Chapter 8** describes making and installing various kinds of binding and purflings.

These small old-style ukuleles have tight radius curves in the waist and around the upper bout. Binding strips need to be bent as accurately as possible to fit the rebates cut around the body edges.

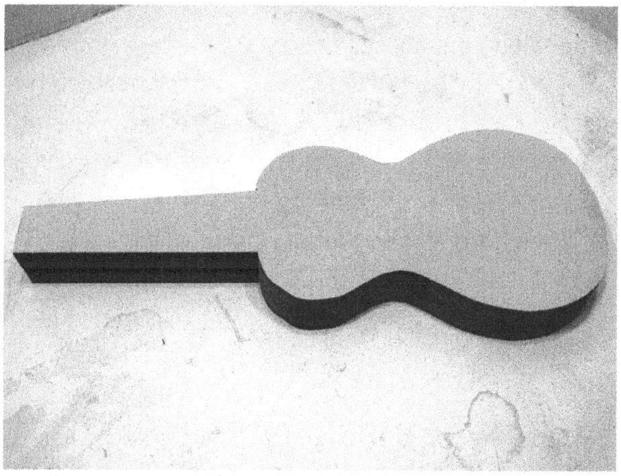

The soundboard clamping caul.

Below: The soundboard roped (and clamped) in place.

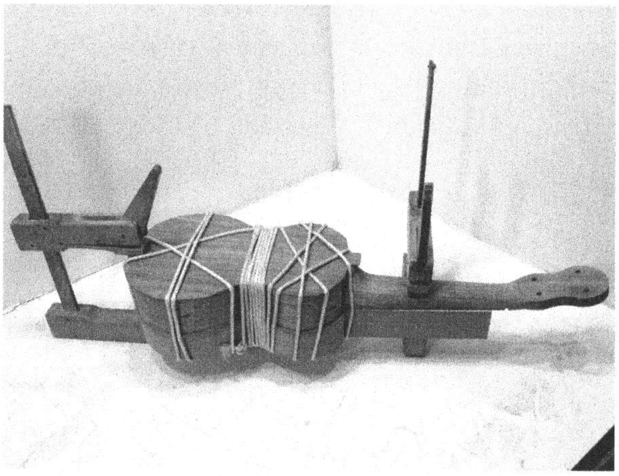

FRETTING

The frets on the original Hawaiian ukuleles would have been 'bar frets', a strip of rectangular-sectioned nickel silver or brass around 1mm x 2mm/0.040 x 0.080". The film shows the builder tapping the frets with a hammer to distort one edge into a 'tang' so it would grip the timber more effectively. Bar fret material can be found, though not very easily, and requires a cleanly cut 1mm x 1mm slot cut into the surface of the neck. Modern T-shaped fretwire is easier to find, and a 50cm/18"length is all that is required. Ukulele/mandolin fretwire is typically around 1.3mm/0.053" wide.

The ukulele ready for fretting.

The frets are inserted directly into the top surface of the neck. It was suggested that the fret slots be cut while the neck was still a right angled block of timber, but if not it will have to be done at this point. The edges along the top of the neck should be a smooth taper from the body to the nut. A sliding bevel can be used to set a consistent angle so the fret slots are cut at 90° to the neck centreline.

Above: The 12th fret is pre-cut to exact length before being hammered into place.

Even if the fret slots were cut earlier, it is likely that the 12th fret slot at the body join has been partially filled by the side, so that slot will need to be re-cut.

Sand the top of the neck/fretboard and the soundboard to 400-grit. Once the frets are inserted, it will be hard to do the finish sanding between the frets. Before inserting the frets it is also useful to bevel the top of the slots slightly with a small triangular file. A shaped support can be made (or a bag of lead shot used) to support the neck under where the frets are being tapped into place with a small hammer. The frets can be cut to slightly longer than is needed and cut to length after being inserted.

Below: A bead of hide glue is wiped into the slots before the frets are inserted and the squeeze-out cleaned up with warm water.

Koa is softer than the usual fingerboard materials if rosewood or ebony and the frets can be hammered in quite easily. Hot animal glue is a useful lubricant for inserting the frets and will also help hold them in place. It can also be cleaned up simply with warm water. Modern aliphatic glues such as Titebond are harder to effectively clean up on the fretboard and can show up later under a finish. File the fret tangs flush with the sides of the neck, and file a bevel on each end of the fret itself.

THE BRIDGE

The bridge on this ukulele is made from a single piece of timber, (an offcut from the neck) 60mm x 15mm x 10mm/2⅜" x ⅝" x ⅜". The finished height of the bridge will be 8mm/5⁄16", and the extra 2mm/3⁄32"thickness to start with allows for four 4mm/5⁄32" holes to be drilled in the back edge for the string knots. Once drilled, the base of the bridge can be sanded or cut away to expose the bottom of the holes. The first part of **Chapter 13** deals with the construction of such a bridge.

The bridge has to be located accurately and pinned into place while being glued. A pencil line was drawn on the soundboard, perpendicular to the centreline, at the calculated saddle position. Two 1⁄16" holes are drilled in the bottom of the bridge, only partially through. Two cut down 1⁄16" brass nails are inserted into the holes so only a short point extends out, the bridge accurately positioned and pushed down to mark the position of the nails. 1⁄16" holes are drilled through the soundboard and the nails replaced by wooden or plastic dowels - toothpicks are good.

The small size of the soundhole and the shallow body can make it hard to get a G-clamp the right size to fit through the soundhole and reach the bridge. An alternative is to insert a chock inside the body that will support the soundboard and back, and allow the use of a couple of wooden cam clamps to be used from the outside. The chock is a short piece of softwood, slightly longer than the distance between the back and soundboard at the bridge position. The piece used was around 30mm/1¼" wide and 6mm/¼" thick and gently wedged so it sat under the bridge. A piece of scrap timber spreads the pressure across the back as glue is applied and the bridge clamped into place. Hide glue is recommended for this, both for strength and ease of cleanup.

FINISHING

Once the glue is dry the entire instruments can be sanded as described in **Chapter 16** and the finish of choice applied.

Below: The bridge, with toothpick locating pins, ready to be glued.

Below: The bridge clamped in place with a supporting chock between the bridge plate and the back.

CHAPTER 12
SHAPING THE NECK

SHAPING THE NECK

The neck of any stringed instrument is a complex three-dimensional object. The neck shaft itself is rounded to fit the hand comfortably and tapers in two directions. At one end it flares into the flat head and at the other expands into the heel. It is the transition between the head, the neck shaft and the heel which are the challenges in carving the neck.

The necks built for these ukuleles have been standardised at 35mm/1⅜"wide at the nut and 45mm/1¾" wide at the 12th fret as well as 13mm/½" deep at the nut and 18mm/¾" deep at the point where the heel starts. This is between the 8th and 9th frets on the 12 frets to the body ukuleles and around the 11th fret on the 14 fret to the body second tenor model and the baritone. The width of the neck is known at these two points and it is possible to draw cross-sections of the neck and calculate facets at tangents to the proposed neck surface. The diagrams on the next page show the process and the widths of the facets to be cut.

Measurements for this procedure are given only in metric. The chart on **page 125** has conversions to both fractions and decimal inches.

As the shape of the neck can get quite complex around the nut, it is easier to start the facet under the first fret. The neck will be a little wider - 36mm rather than 35mm and slightly deeper - 13.5mm instead of 13mm. Mark the edge points of the facets on the side and back of the neck. 4mm down from the bottom of the fretboard at the 1st fret and 6.5mm at the 18mm thickness point. On the back of the neck the facets start 9mm from the centreline under the 1st fret and 10mm at the 18mm point.

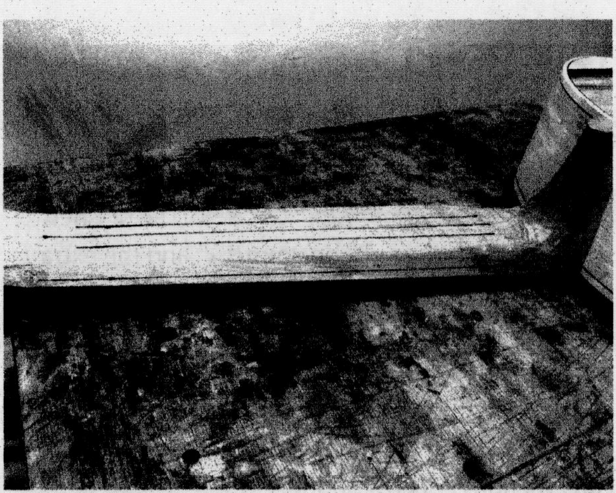

The primary facets marked on the rectangular neck shaft.

The primary facets carved into the neck.

Carve the facet into each side of the neck so the neck has five surfaces: a flat section under each edge of the fingerboard, another flat section along the centre of the back of the neck and two sections at an angle between them as shown in the photograph above.

Mark the secondary facets as shown in the lower two diagrams below and carve those away. This will leave five facets on each side of the neck and once the high points are carved or sanded away the shaft of the neck will be close to finalised. A piece of 80-grit paper on a cork sanding block used across the grain is efficient and quick.

NOTE: *The images are of the baritone ukulele built in the Spanish style with an integral neck, used because the neck is made from a light coloured timber and the facet lines more visible. The same methodology is used for an integral or a separate neck.*

The challenge of neck carving is to smoothly join the carved heel and the shaped head to the main shaft of the neck. It is a complex three-dimensional object and optimally, all the lines should blend smoothly together. The best way to get a sense of how the curves come together is to look tangentially across the neck while rotating the instrument along its lengthwise axis. As the neck shaft flares at both the head and the heel any lumpy bits will be come quickly obvious. These can be corrected with a chisel, sanding blocks or a scraper.

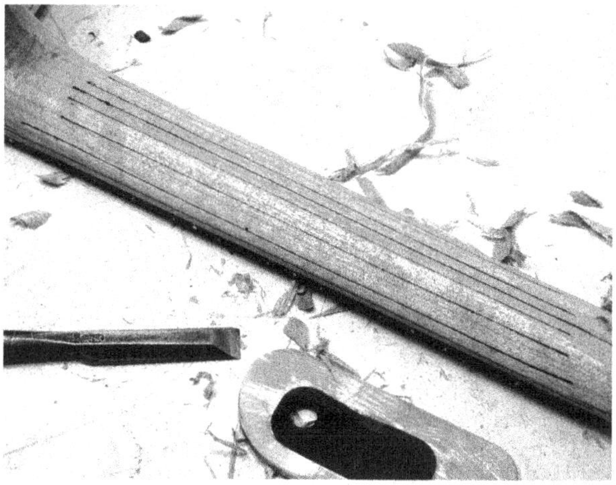

The secondary facets marked after the first facets have been carved.

Once the neck is smooth, the entire instrument can be sanded preparatory to applying whatever finish is chosen. It is suggested that successively finer grits up to 280 or 320-grit are used to remove scratches from coarser grits or tool marks. A suggested progression is 80, 120, 180, and 280/320-grit paper, although on softwood soundboards the coarsest grade should be 120-grit.

Marking the facets at the first fret (on the left) and on the right at the point where the neck flares into the heel, between the 8th & 9th frets for a 12 fret to the body ukulele or between the 10th & 11th frets for a 14 fret to the body instrument. On a 14 fret instrument the neck will be slightly wider at this point, but the difference when shaping the neck is negligible.

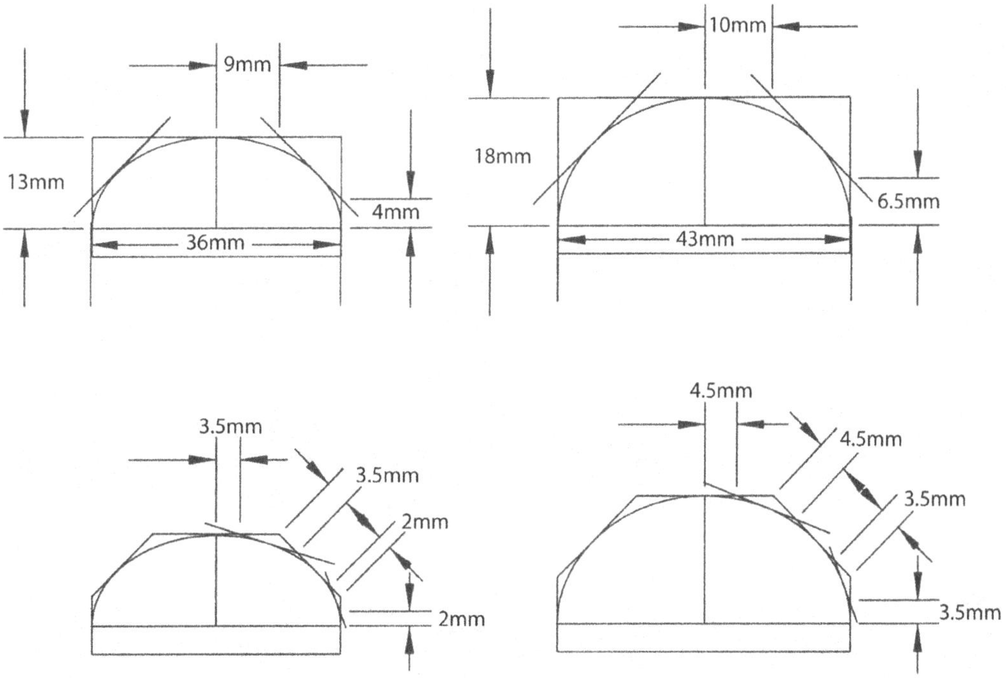

CHAPTER 13
BRIDGES

The ukulele bridge is the all important connection between the strings and the instrument's body. It acts as the anchoring point for the strings, either tied on directly or passing through to be knotted underneath the soundboard. The bridge has to be glued strongly enough to resist the pull of the strings trying to tear it off the soundboard. It also acts as an extra soundboard brace, stiffening that central area of the lower half of the soundboard.

Some of the early Hawaiian made ukuleles used a guitar-style pin bridge, but most quickly adopted a uncomplicated rectangular bridge to which the strings were attached by a knot or a loop.

A MINIMALIST ONE PIECE BRIDGE

At their simplest ukulele bridges are a single piece of hardwood 60mm/2 3/8" long, 15mm/5/8" wide and 6mm/1/4" thick with a extra 2mm/3/32" ridge along the front edge which acts as a saddle. Many of the early Hawaiian ukuleles fixed the strings using either a rebate cut into the back bottom edge of the bridge or four small holes drilled in the back of the bridge.

The rebate is cut around 4mm/5/32" deep and 2mm/3/32" high along the back bottom edge starting 6mm/1/4" in from the ends.

The four holes at 14mm/9/16" centres are drilled 5mm/3/16" deep using a 4mm/3/32" brad-point bit. If the holes are used start with a block 10mm/3/8" deep and then cut or sand away the bottom of the bridge so that bottom 1mm/1/32" of each hole is exposed on the finished bridge. The centre of the holes should be 1mm/1/32" above the eventual bottom of the bridge.

Above: Four holes for the string knots drilled into the bridge block.

Below: The block thinned so the bottom edges of the holes are exposed.

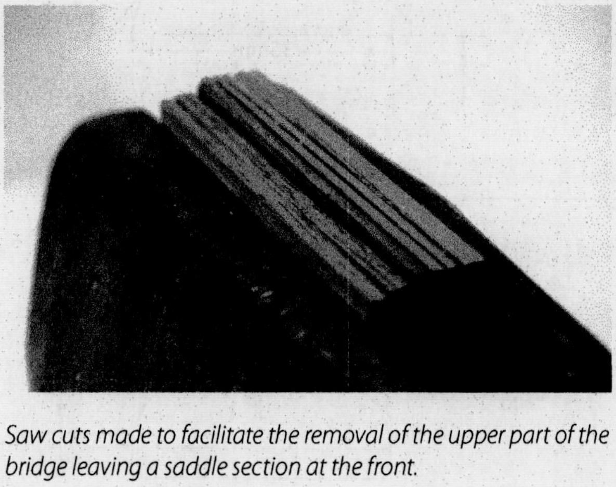

Saw cuts made to facilitate the removal of the upper part of the bridge leaving a saddle section at the front.

The saddle is simply a raised ridge 2mm/3⁄32" high on the front edge. A Stewart-MacDonald fret slotting saw with a depth stop allows several cuts to be made behind the saddle to allow the shelf behind the saddle to be consistent. The waste can be chiselled away, slots for the strings cut into the previously drilled holes and the saddle smoothed off.

Four narrow slots are then cut from the rebate or the holes at the same 14mm/11⁄16" centres, at an angle towards the saddle. Knots tied in the strings lock the string ends into the rebate or holes.

A SEPARATE SADDLE

A more sophisticated, and height adjustable bridge replaces the integral saddle with a separate saddle made from bone or ebony. Saddles are commonly 3⁄32" wide and bone blanks are available from luthier suppliers. The front of the slot is 5mm/3⁄16" from the front of the bridge and cut or routed 3mm/1⁄8" deep. A few minutes with a router table can cut enough bridge slots for many ukuleles. The saddle slots could also be cut with a fine-toothed handsaw using wooden blocks to ensure straight and vertical cuts. The waste would be cut or scraped out with a narrow chisel and the bottom of the slot smoothed with an appropriately sized file.

The 60mm/23⁄8" length of the bridge is fine for soprano and concert sized instruments, but the wider tenor and baritone soundboard require a larger bridge - 100mm/4" long. Only the centre section need be 6mm/1⁄4" thick. From a point 5mm/3⁄16" past the outer strings, the thickness can curve down to 2-3mm/3⁄32-1⁄8" thick at the ends. Alternatively the centre section can finish with straight cuts and 'wings' like those on a classical guitar bridge can be carved from the outside sections.

The finished bridge with slots cut for the strings. The knots are captured in the drilled holes and the slots lead the strings up over the saddle.

Routing a 3⁄32" slot in a rosewood block. The block is long enough for several ukulele bridges.

Below: Toothpicks used to locate the bridge for gluing.

Below: The oversize routed bridge blank.

ATTACHING THE STRINGS

TIE BLOCK BRIDGE

These bridges use a tie-block at the back of the bridge, in the manner of classical guitar bridges. This requires the bridge itself to be wider, a minimum of 22mm/⅞″, which allows a tie-block 10mm/⅜″ wide. A second cut is made 5mm/3⁄16″ behind the saddle slot to the same 3mm/⅛″ depth and the timber behind the saddle slot is cut away to ramp down to the bottom of the second cut which is the front of the tie-block. 1.5mm/1⁄16″ holes are drilled from the back of the bridge at 14mm/9⁄16″ centres so they emerge right at the lowest point of the ramp behind the saddle. The upper edges of the tie-block can be reenforced with thin strips of bone or something similar to prevent the strings from digging in.

Above: A tie-block style bridge under construction showing the second routed slot behind the saddle slot.

Below: String holes being drilled in the back of a tie-block bridge.

STRING THROUGH BRIDGE

A simple and elegant approach is simply to drill four 1.5mm/1⁄16″ holes through the bridge, soundboard and bridge plate at 14mm/9⁄16″ centres. The strings can be fed in from the top and the ends pulled out through the soundhole to be knotted around a glass or ceramic bead and then pulled back inside before being fitted to the tuners.

PIN BRIDGE

Pin bridges are used most often for steel-string guitars, though they were originally used on 19th century classical guitars from Northern Europe. The bridge has tapered holes drilled through at the usual 14mm/9⁄16″ centres. The strings are fitted with a ball of some kind on the end which bears on a hardwood bridgeplate inside the instrument, while the tapered pin stops the ball popping out the hole. When fitted properly, pin-bridges certainly work. A tie- or a string-through bridge is a simpler and just as effective a solution for a ukulele unless the builder has experience with steel-string guitar construction.

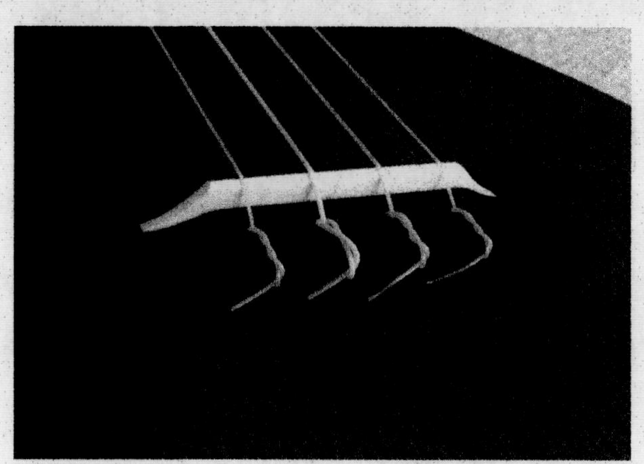

A wider tie-block bridge on a tenor ukulele showing the technique of looping the strings in place.

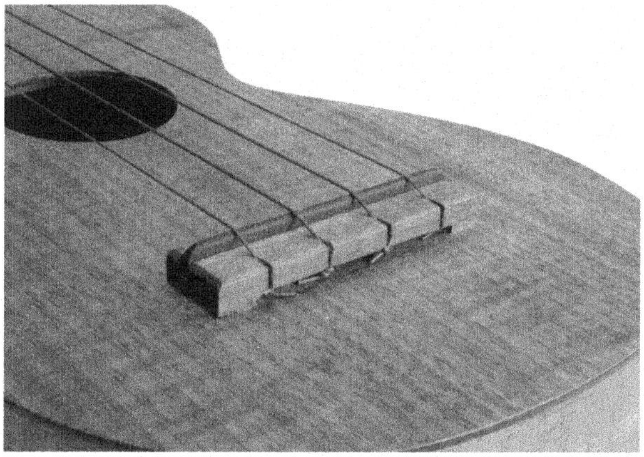

A simple bridge with a separate ebony saddle and a rebate for the string knots.

Above: A simple bridge with holes drilled through the bridge and soundboard. The strings are inserted from the top and brought out the soundhole before being tied around small beads.

Below: A pin bridge on a tenor ukulele.

GLUING THE BRIDGE

Gluing the bridge, especially on smaller sized ukuleles, can be a delicate operation. The bridge has to be precisely placed and firmly glued. Most of the bridge types described above use a separate 3⁄32″ wide saddle.

A simple jig made from acrylic sheet 5-6mm/3⁄16-1⁄4″ thick can be used to accurately position the bridge. The acrylic is cut to the outline of the fretboard extending to the bridge position with a smaller piece of 3mm/1⁄8″ acrylic glued at the narrow end that will fit in the nut slot. Two small pieces of 3⁄32″ wide material, that will fit into the saddle slot of the bridge, are inset the appropriate distance from the nut. Two 1⁄16″ holes are drilled on the line of the saddle to allow the bridge to be pinned before gluing. A centreline on the jig will help keep the bridge centred.

If the ukulele has been fretted according to the Rule of 18, the contact point of the bridge saddle will be the scale length from the nut. That contact point should be 1⁄32″ back from the front of the saddle. If the fret positions have been calculated by dividing by 17.817, 2mm/5⁄64″ should be added to the theoretical string length to position the bridge saddle.

The jig can be clamped over the fretboard, aligned with the edges, allowing the bridge to be positioned on the centreline of the instrument

Once the bridge is positioned correctly the two holes should be drilled for the locating pins. 1⁄16″ brass nails or wooden toothpicks (which are often 1⁄16″ in diameter) can be used for this.

For the simple one piece bridge used on the Old Style soprano, two 1⁄16″ blind holes can be drilled in the bottom of the bridge and 1⁄16″ nails inserted, cut down so just the point extends out of the bottom of the bridge. Mark the bridge position with masking tape on the front and each end. Press the bridge into position so the protruding nails each mark a hole and drill holes for two pieces of cut-off toothpicks.

The bridge can be glued with hot hide glue or aliphatic resin. It will need to be clamped in place until the glue sets. There will almost inevitably be some glue squeeze-out around the edges of the bridge. This needs to be thoroughly cleaned up before the glue sets completely. Warm water, paper towels, toothpicks and small screw-drivers can all be useful and the clamps may have to be removed sequentially to allow access.

Wooden locating pins will need to be cut away and a narrow 1⁄16" - 3⁄32" wide blade may need to be fabricated to cleanly cut the pins off at the bottom of the saddle slot. Brass nails may need the heat of a soldering iron to soften the glue to allow their removal.

With smaller sized ukuleles there can be a problem with finding appropriately sized clamps, and fitting even one in through the small soundhole. Vacuum clamping is one alternative, but does require a vacuum pump and a purpose made flexible caul to let atmospheric pressure do its work. Alternatively a piece of scrap timber can be fitted as a prop between the soundboard and back under the bridge and a couple of wooden cam clamps used to clamp the bridge from outside. The support block should be long enough to just fit between the underside of the bridge patch and the back and be around 4cm x 1cm/1½" x ⅜".

Above: Two cast aluminium G-clamps used to glue a pin bridge on a tenor ukulele. The clamps are fitted around the fan braces.

Below: Two longer cam clamps and a single cast aluminium clamp for the baritone bridge. Again the clamps fit around the fan braces.

Below: The bridge locating jig for a 34cm/13.5" scale soprano ukulele. A separate jig will need to made for each size of ukulele built.

CHAPTER 14
TUNERS

There are several styles of tuners that are used on ukuleles, ranging from wooden pegs to highly engineered worm-gear tuners.

Wooden violin-style pegs and metal friction tuners are direct 1:1 tuners, which can make fine adjustments tricky. Planetary-geared tuners, such as Pegheds and the Gotoh UPT models are a 4:1 ratio which makes fine adjustments easier. Worm and gear tuners are usually either 14:1 or 16:1 ratio. This is good for steel strings but more than is required for stretchier nylon strings.

Whatever style of tuners are chosen, the holes are drilled during the initial shaping and thicknessing of the head. They are fitted after all finishing and polishing is completed.

WOODEN PEGS

The early Hawaiian ukuleles used violin style tuning pegs which, when properly fitted and installed, work perfectly well with low tension strings. A good quality 30:1 taper peg cutter and a reamer are necessary to fit violin pegs properly with the peg cutter adjusted to match the reamer before use. They

Test fitting a peg.

Above: Drilling the hole through the peg for the string.
Below: The pegs fitted and ready for strings.

Below: Reaming a peg hole with a 30:1 tapered reamer.

are not cheap, but they will last for years. For ukuleles ½ or ¾ size pegs are needed. Violin pegs can be bought pre-tapered, but usually benefit from being run through the cutter to true up any deviance.

Before inserting the peg in the cutter a knife is used to score a line around the bottom of the raised collar that is turned just below the button. This will prevent the collar being chipped on the end of the peg-cutter blade. The peg is then inserted into the cutter gently and turned clockwise so the blade takes a fine cut. After a couple of turns back the peg out, clear the waste and check to see if the peg is cleanly and uniformly cut. Repeat the cutting if necessary. A well set-up cutter should leave the peg smooth enough not to need sanding, but very fine (280-grit and up) paper could be used carefully to remove any roughness.

Once the peg is smoothly tapered ream out the pilot hole in the head slowly and incrementally from the back. When finally seated there should be about 10mm/⅜" of the shaft visible at the back of the head and 10mm/⅜" protruding on the face. Excess length on the face of the head can be trimmed back, but if the hole is over-reamed all the rest will have to be altered to match.

A hole for the string is drilled 4mm/5/32" from the end of the peg. This will allow the string to wrap around the peg below the hole. A 25mm/1" (approximately, the exact size does not matter) square block of scrap timber can be used to hold the peg under a drill press. Drill a pilot hole near one edge and ream it out so the end of the peg just pokes out the other side. Plane or sand away the block at the angle of the taper so when inserted, the peg is visible. The block will hold the peg horizontal in the drill press so a 1/16" hole can be drilled. A smear of violin peg dope will help the smooth turning of the pegs.

METAL FRICTION PEGS

These were an invention of the 1880s for gut strung banjos and quickly adopted by the Chicago factories for ukuleles after 1915. They use a metal screw to clamp two sections of the tuner to the head and have changed little, if at all, in 130 years.

Grover friction pegs on a soprano ukulele.

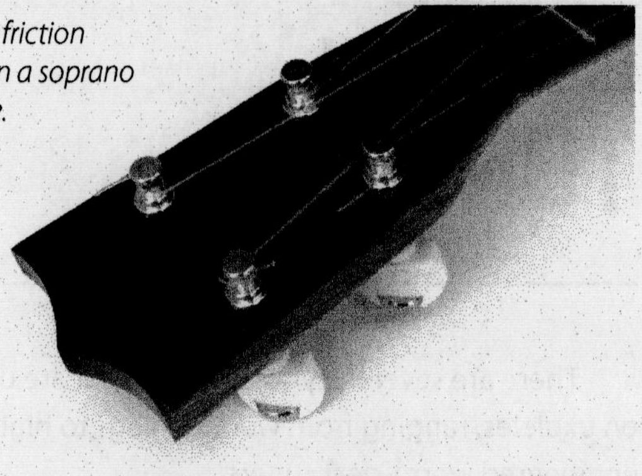

Friction pegs do work remarkably well for low tension ukulele strings, are simple to install and require little or no maintenance other than periodically checking the tension screw. Grover, Gotoh and Waverly are recommended brands.

VIOLIN PLANETARY TUNERS

Some clever engineering has managed to fit 4:1 geared planetary tuning machines inside what looks like a wooden peg. These were originally conceived for bowed instruments, but there are now models made by the American manufacturer Pegheds which fit ukuleles and guitars. A fine screw thread is moulded on the shaft where it passes through the head. They are supplied with two right and two left hand threads. They need to be installed by screwing them into the head in the direction which would normally loosen the strings. They need a tapered reamer to fit them, and the hole must be reamed very carefully so the last 2-3mm of the threads cut into the wood when screwed into place with fingers alone. A drop of wood glue on the thread is used to help lock them into place.

They work with an ingenious variable friction so when the button is pushed in the tuners tighten and effectively lock the tuners. Pulling the button out a little loosens the mechanism.

Internally geared Pegheds fitted to a soprano ukulele.

METAL PLANETARY TUNERS

Planetary tuners were introduced in the 1920s during the banjo boom as a much improved way to cope with the increased tension of steel strings. The Japanese tuner manufacturer Gotoh makes lightweight 4:1 planetary tuners (model designation UPT) specifically for ukuleles in a variety of finishes and button styles. GraphTech makes Tune-A-Lele planetary tuners on the same principle with a 6:1 ratio.

WORM GEAR TUNERS

Most manufacturers of worm and pinion-gear guitar tuners include ukulele tuners in their range. There are cheap ones from China which cost a couple of dollars or intricately machined models which will cost $100 or more for a set. Grover, Gotoh, Schaller, Rubner and Waverly all make good quality tuners which are readily available. A $25 set of nickel plated Grover or Gotoh tuners with plastic buttons will work perfectly well in most situations, but will not look nearly as cool as a set of Waverlys with ebony buttons or the ultra-lightweight Gotoh Stealth models, both of which are four times more expensive than the basic Grover tuners.

Gotoh UPT planetary tuners.

Gotoh worm-gear tuners.

CHAPTER 15
FINISHING & SET-UP

The use of clear finishes on fretted instruments is constantly evolving. The idea of all finishes is to protect the timber from moisture and bodily fluids, as well as to enhance the appearance of the instrument in a way that does not adversely affect the production of sound. Some finishes have centuries of use while others have been developed in the past decade. The choice of finish will depend on the expectations of the builder, as well as access to methods of applying the finish. It is probably impractical to expect to have a spray booth in a high-rise apartment, but applying French Polish or wipe-on drying oil is very possible.

The secret of any clear finishes is knowing how to prepare the timber surface and how to apply whatever finish is chosen. Some are easier to use than others, but all require a learning curve to get the best results.

The intent of the first part of this chapter is not to delve into the detail of applying any of the possible finishes. It is more to outline the options available and the processes involved. The following section looks at the various kinds of finish in a rough order of ease of use and application in a home workshop.

CHOICE OF FINISH

DRYING OILS

There is a wide range of drying oil wood finishes available. Pure tung oil is from the nut of the tung tree (*Aleurites fordii* - sometimes *Vernicia fordii*) and has been used by Chinese woodworkers for centuries. Many of the products sold as Tung Oil finishes may only contain a small percentage of tung oil, and are more like the various Scandinavian or Danish Oil finishes which are a mix of oils, a resin (usually a polyurethane) and a thinner. Check the can or bottle for the ingredients. *Tru-Oil* is a linseed oil based finish which was originally used for gun-stocks but which is used widely for musical instruments.

The liquid soaks slightly into the wood and hardens as it dries. It can be applied with a piece of cloth or 0000 steel wool and then rubbed off as it becomes tacky. One coat a day for 3 or 4 days builds up a soft gloss. When used on an open grained timber the pore structure will be very obvious. It is not forgiving of careless sanding and the wood should be sanded to at least 320-grit before the first coat. Other than that it is simple to apply, almost foolproof.

Plus - ease of application (just wipe it on and rub it off), repairable.
Minus - does not have the smooth look of a lacquer and shows up any carelessness in sanding.

FRENCH POLISH OR SPIRIT VARNISH

"French Polish" is used to describe both the shellac based varnish and the rubbing technique used to apply it. In its simplest form the varnish is shellac flakes dissolved in alcohol, while commercially available French Polish usually has one or more drying oils or resins added to make the dried polish a little softer and more flexible. There are also various formulas available to make spirit varnishes in the workshop from shellac and various additives. Traditionally it is applied with a 'rubber', a pad of soft cloth that is saturated with the polish and then wrapped in another piece of cloth. This is applied in a circular rubbing motion which leaves a thin coat of polish with each application. It can also be sprayed, but it uses a lot more polish.

Plus - cheap, easy low-tech application, easily touched up or repaired.
Minus - can be marked by moisture and skin contact, especially where a forearm comes in contact with the soundboard.

HARD SHELLAC

This is de-waxed blond shellac to which is added a chemical which hardens the finish, so it is impervious to moisture (sweat, beer etc). It can be used in the same way as ordinary shellac (french polishing or spraying), but after about three weeks changes chemically to form a much harder coating. It is available from Shines (who developed it) and U-Beaut in Australia with a similar (perhaps identical) product sold in America as Royal-Lac.

Plus - ease of application, non-toxic.
Minus - not much.

WATERBASED VARNISH

Since the 1980s there have been an increasing number of water based varnishes available. These are based on acrylic or polyurethane resins dissolved in a solvent which is then mixed with water. The water and the solvent evaporate and the clear resin is left as the coating. These water based varnishes have had a mixed acceptance. Some like them because of their relatively non-toxic nature and ease of application. The water based varnishes can be sprayed or brushed.

Plus - simple low technology brush application.
Minus - a plastic or sometimes a slightly milky appearance.

OIL VARNISH

Varnish can be a catch-all term for a range of both oil and water based brushable clear timber coatings. A century ago 'varnish' was an oil-based alkyd resin cooked up with an oil which dried, eventually, on contact with air. It was thinned with mineral spirits (mineral turpentine). Varnishes for external use, such as 'spar varnish' used on boats, used a high proportion of oil and stayed relatively soft and flexible. Furniture varnishes used about a tenth the amount of oil for the same amount of resin and dried much harder. These could be polished to a high gloss after some weeks of drying. The more modern (and now more commonly available) versions have polyurethane resin added to the alkyd resin and usually sold as 'polyurethane'. They are still thinned with mineral spirits/turpentine.

Plus - simple low technology brush application.
Minus - a long drying time, successive coats do not 'burn in' to previous layers.

SPRAYING LACQUER

Nitro-cellulose lacquer has been around since early last century and is essentially plant cellulose dissolved in nitric acid and thinned with rather nasty hydrocarbon solvents. It needs to be sprayed, as the solvent thinners evaporate too quickly to allow brushing. It was been the industry standard finish for many upper end instruments since the 1920s though replaced in most production environments by synthetic resin lacquers or UV cured coatings. Nitro-cellulose lacquer needs to be applied in multiple coats as around 85% of what is sprayed on evaporates away. Nitro lacquer is available in varying degrees of gloss. 100% gloss requires perfect preparation and grain filling while a 10% gloss satin finish is a lot more forgiving. A workable finish can be obtained by just a few double coats over a day or two, a light sanding the next day with 400-grit paper followed by a wash-coat of pure thinners.

Plus - clear, flexible finish that can be retouched or repaired.
Minus - needs spray equipment, thinners quite toxic and may annoy neighbours, multiple coats needed, takes several weeks to fully cure.

PREPARATION

The first decision to be made is how polished the ukulele needs to be. A simple drying oil finish can be completed in a few days with minimal equipment, and most of that time is waiting for the finish to harden. A full-gloss lacquer finish will take several weeks to complete with much more equipment and time involved.

The first step is sanding, a process interspersed with filling the grain of open pored timbers as well as filling any gaps that appear around not quite perfectly fitting binding. The grain-filling can be ignored for a flat or semi-gloss finish, but does look better to fill any noticeable gaps around the binding. The eye gets drawn to such gaps and they can be very difficult to fill with the finish itself.

The secret to a good finish is to have as smooth as possible a surface over which the finish is applied. This means sanding the timber with increasingly finer grades of sandpaper to progressively remove the scratches of coarser grades. It is suggested in previous chapters on assembling the ukuleles that 80- or 120-grit sandpaper paper is a good starting point to eventually achieve a smooth, scratch-free surface. It should be remembered that the body of most ukuleles in made of timber no more than 1.5-2mm/0.060-.080" thick and vigorously applied 80-grit sandpaper can thin that down rather quickly.

The suggested sequence is 80-, 120-, 180- and 280 or 320-grit using aluminium oxide sandpaper for hardwoods. Finer grades run the risk of burnishing the timber as much as sanding it and possibly causing adhesion problems with sprayed lacquer finishes. The sandpaper should be non-stearated. Stearate is a metallic soap added to sandpaper as a lubricant and may also cause problems with finish adhesion.

After sanding to 120-grit the soundboard, back and sides should be smooth, without ripples, and with the corners of the bindings smoothly curving from the sides to the back and top plates, especially if rope binding has been used. The neck shaft should be straight without lumps and flare smoothly to the head and heel. Sanding with 180-grit should remove any obvious scratches from previous, coarser grades.

GAP AND GRAIN FILLING

Any filling of the grain and gaps should be done at this stage. Go over the body and neck with a stiff brush and/or compressed air (a spray gun without the fluid container works well) to get rid of all the dust. Check for any gaps around the bindings. They will need to be filled with a filler made from sanding dust and a binding agent. The dust should be produced by sanding a scrap of the same wood with a slightly worn piece of 180-grit sandpaper.

The binding agent can be wood glue, shellac, or clear lacquer. Thinned nitro-cellulose lacquer is especially effective with spruce or other light coloured woods as the dried mixture stays much the same colour as the original dust. Blond de-waxed shellac works almost as well, while wood glue tends to produce a darker coloured filler than the original dust. Some experimentation is suggested on pieces of scrap timber before using any filler on the ukulele itself.

Such fillers can take a couple of days to dry and stop shrinking back, especially if lacquer is used as the binder. A couple of applications may be necessary.

Grain filling of open-pored timbers, which is most hardwoods, can be done in several ways. The traditional method for classical guitars uses powdered pumice (an aerated volcanic rock) rubbed, with a little alcohol, onto the surface of the wood which has been sealed with shellac. The abrasive qualities of the pumice form a wood/shellac/pumice slurry which fills the grain of the timber very effectively.

Coloured paste fillers are available in both oil and water based formulations. The oil based fillers, thinned with mineral spirits (known as white spirits in the UK or mineral turpentine in Australia) are applied and rubbed off with a coarse cloth and need a couple of days to fully dry. The water-based paste fillers dry more quickly but will need more sanding afterwards. The colour chosen should be a shade or two darker than the timber to be filled. Most manufacturers have a range of colours to match commonly used timbers but some adjustment of the colour may be required using wood stain.

An alternative to coloured paste grain fillers is using a clear filler, either epoxy or a clear water-based gel. Any 30 minute wood-working epoxy can be used, but it is messy and will require sanding after the epoxy is fully cured. Application is done with a blade or spatula such as an old credit card, working the resin into the pores of the timber. There are two schools of thought on epoxy sealer/fillers. One is to leave a film of epoxy all over, and the other involves sanding down to bare wood, only leaving the epoxy in the pores. For the first technique it is important not to sand through to bare wood as it will look different under the final finish, while the drawback of the second approach is that the sanding back to the wood can expose new, unfilled pores. Application of the epoxy to the end grain of the neck heel might require thinning the epoxy with alcohol or acetone.

The water based clear fillers are a relatively new introduction to the field and are applied with a brush or spatula onto timber sealed with shellac. They can be sanded flat after only a couple of hours and ready for the top coats the next day.

The main lutherie supply companies stock suitable epoxy and water based clear grain fillers.

PREPARING FOR THE TOP COATS OF THE FINISH

The marks left on the timber after 280- or 320-grit sandpaper should not be visible under a clear finish if the sanding was done carefully and methodically, although a softwood soundboard can benefit from going to 360- or 400-grit. In any case, a light spray with water from a laundry hand sprayer will show up any scratches immediately and these can be sanded out after the water has evaporated.

The fingerboard should be masked off with masking tape, carefully sealing along both edges and around the frets. The tape should extend into the nut slot and over the soundhole end of the board.

The interior of the body should be vacuumed and/or blown clean of dust and shavings. The ukulele needs to be held in some way while the finish coats are applied. If the neck and body are joined, a small F or bar-clamp can be fitted through the soundhole and clamped to the end of the fingerboard (if it extends that far).

If spraying the finish coats, the clamp handle allows the ukuleles to be rotated for even coverage and then hung up to dry. If a clamp through the soundhole is impractical the instrument may be held with a wire hook through the two upper tuner mounting holes. The head can be sprayed first, the wire hooks inserted and held while spraying the rest of the body.

For wipe-on or brushed finishes the neck and body can be done while holding the other end of the instrument.

If the neck and body are to be finished separately, as with a bolt-on neck, wooden handles can be attached using the insert(s) and holes drilled for the attachment bolt(s).

A sponge rubber block the depth of the body (or something similar) is inserted into the soundhole and covered with a disk cut from cardboard that is of slightly greater diameter than the soundhole. Give body and neck a final blow with compressed air and/or a wipe down with tack-cloth to remove any remaining dust.

THE TOP COATS

Each kind of finish requires different techniques for application and final polishing. Often that technique will vary a little between different brands of the same kind of finish. Experiment first on offcuts to get a feel for how the finish is applied and then polished.

THE SET-UP

The final part of building an ukulele is the 'set-up' which will turn the little wooden box into a musical instrument. This includes:
- Levelling, re-crowning and polishing the frets,
- fitting the tuners,
- making and fitting the nut and saddle,
- attaching the strings and tuning the instrument.

FRETS

However carefully the frets were hammered or pressed into the fingerboard slots, almost inevitably there will be slight discrepancies in the height of the frets above the fingerboard surface. This can lead to the strings buzzing on adjacent frets or, in the worst case, the string actually being stopped at another, higher, fret.

The tops of the frets need to be level along the length of the strings. If there is a slight radius sanded into the fingerboard surface, with a matching curve to the frets, the levelling should follow that transverse curve as well. The levelling can be done with several abrasive tools, such as a medium-cut flat file, an unused carborundum sharpening stone or one of the specifically designed tools available from suppliers such as Stewart-MacDonald or Luthiers Mercantile.

Before levelling the tops of the frets check that each fret is solidly in its slot, especially at the ends. Press down on each fret end to feel for any movement. If a fret is loose, clamp the end down and wick in a drop of cyanoacrylate glue (aka Super Glue or CA glue)and leave clamped until it dries.

The levelling tool is applied up and down the fingerboard, paralleling the direction of the strings, with the aim to get a flat strip across the entire length of each fret. An oblique light source can be helpful in seeing the newly machined flat sections or a contrasting coloured marker pen can be used across the length of each fret. The aim is to get the smallest possible flat bit on each fret to minimise the loss of fret height, so check after every pass or so to see how the levelling is going and stop as soon as the last flat section appears. The ends of each fret should be bevelled at a 35-40° angle, with the bevel just extending onto the edge of the fingerboard itself.

The original semi-circular cross-section of the frets now needs to be reshaped with a fret file. This is a small file with a hollow to match the width of the fret and available in various sizes to match common fret sizes. The file should be applied along each fret until the flat section is only just visible. The bevelled ends of the frets should also be filed to take off the sharp edges of the bevel. The rounding of the frets can also be done with 400-grit wet and dry sandpaper if the specialised file is not available.

The file marks and the remainder of the flat sections can be removed by sanding successively with 400-, 600- and 1200-grit wet and dry paper and then polished. The sanding can go along and across the frets to remove all file or levelling marks. A metal polish such as Brasso is effective for the final polishing but lutherie suppliers also offer other ways of doing this. For ukuleles with flush fingerboards, made from koa or other lighter colour timber fingerboards, the timber surface should be protected with masking tape before levelling and polishing.

TUNERS

Appropriately sized holes should have already been drilled in the peg head for the chosen tuners. The holes may need cleaning to remove any accumulation of finish which can make then just that little bit too small. This can be done with a reamer or round file, taking care not to chip any hard lacquer on the top or back surface. A slight bevel can be machined with a countersink bit to clean the edges.

As mentioned in the section on tuner types, the planetary-geared violin style tuners need a carefully reamed tapered hole to fit the tuners at the right depth.

NUT AND SADDLE

The nut width and bridge string spacing on all the ukuleles described in this book has been kept the same, 35mm/1⅜" for the nut with the strings 9mm/¹¹⁄₃₂" apart centre-to-centre and the strings

14mm/9⁄16" apart at the bridge. The actual length of the saddle will depend on which bridge design is chosen. A standard nut width of 3mm/⅛" and a saddle width of 3⁄32" are suggested as these are a standard size of nut and saddle blanks available from suppliers.

This is one part of building a ukulele where the tools designed specifically for the job - a set of dedicated nut slotting files - are very useful. though a set of jeweller's files can do the job if necessary. The important thing is that the slots are the same size as the strings.

Nuts and saddles can be made from a variety of materials. Bone or a synthetic material such as Tusq or Micarta can be used, or scrap pieces of ebony can be machined to the suggested thicknesses. There are also specialty suppliers who can supply more exotic materials such as fossilised mammoth ivory or mother of pearl.

The nut blank should be trimmed to the correct length and fitted into the slot without glue. Using a pencil, mark the approximate height of the nut which will be a little over 2mm/3⁄32" above the fretboard surface - a little more than the fret height and the thickness of the thickest string - and sand to the line. Mark the string slot positions and file shallow slots with the appropriately sized nut files. There should be equal space left outside of the 1st and 4th string slots.

Cut the saddle blank to the required length and fit into the slot. Mark a line 3mm/⅛" above the top of the bridge and sand the blank to almost that mark.

STRINGS

There are many different brands of ukulele strings and most have sets available for the various sizes and string lengths of ukuleles. Often a particular ukulele will respond better with one type of string or another, so some experimentation may be needed.

The first process is to attach the strings to the bridge and this will be different depending on which style of bridge has been used. The simple bridge with a slot or holes at the back will need knots to be tied on the end of the string to anchor the string to the bridge.

A tie-bridge will need the string to be looped through the holes on the back of the bridge and back around the string to lock it in place in the same manner as a classical guitar.

A pin bridge will need knots tied in the string ends so the knots will be jammed onto the bridge plate in front of the pins themselves. The knots may have to be quite large to prevent them pulling up past the pins, or small glass, ceramic or plastic beads may be used. This may depend of the size of the bridge pins.

A string-through bridge will need a bead securely tied to the end of each string to hold it in place. The string should be fed through the bridge and fished out of the soundhole for the bead to be tied in place.

Pull the strings finger tight to the tuner posts and tie the strings in a looped knot to the posts. Tighten the strings to pitch. They will stretch and drop out of tune quickly but should become stable with a few re-tunings.

FINAL ADJUSTMENTS

The nut slots can now be filed to the correct depth. The slots should slope towards the head at a little less than the angle of the strings and be deep enough so when the string is pushed to the fingerboard between the second and third frets the string just clears the first fret by the thickness of a sheet of paper. There should be an audible 'tink' when the string is tapped down onto the first fret whilst being held down in front of the second fret. The height of the nut should then be trimmed so the depth of the slots are a little less than the thickness of the strings and the ends rounded over from the top of the fingerboard to the outside slots with a file or 180-grit sandpaper. The rear edge of the nut can be rounded over and the nut polished in the same way as the frets with increasingly finer grits.

With a 3-4mm/⅛-5⁄32" thick fingerboard, a correctly slotted nut and a 6mm/¼" high bridge with the saddle protruding another 3mm/⅛", the strings should be be around 3mm/8⁄64" (⅛") above the 12th fret. The string height above the frets is known as the 'action' and determines how comfortable the instrument is to play. If the action is to low the strings will buzz on adjacent frets. If too high the ukulele will be harder to play and pushing the frets down to the frets will stretch the strings to a sharper pitch.

3mm/9/64" (1/8") at the 12th fret is a good string height to aim for. 64ths of an inch are useful increments to work with, as a change of 1/32" at the saddle will move the action at the 12th fret by 1/64". Changing the action by a sixty-fourth or two is often all that is necessary to make a comfortably playing ukulele. Once the profile of the top of the saddle is set, it simpler to remove any excess height by sanding the bottom edge , taking care to keep it flat and square. A disk sander is the quickest way to do this but 180-grit sandpaper on a flat surface is also very effective.

Once the correct saddle height is established, round over the top of the saddle with 180-grit sandpaper keeping the contact point for the strings no more than a third of the width from the front of the saddle. The ends can be rounded over, in a similar way as done to the nut and the entire saddle polished as much as is desired.

PICKUPS AND ELECTRONICS

Pickups are sometimes fitted to ukuleles so they can be amplified for use on stage. There is some information on types of pickups and pre-amplifiers that can be used with a ukulele on **page 145**.

Measuring the action at the 12th fret with a small ruler. The height of the strings above the fret is the hoped-for 9/64" (1/8").

Filing a nut slot at an angle between the plane of the fretboard and that of the head.

Above: The completed nut with strings fitted.

Below: Strings looped and locked around the tieblock.

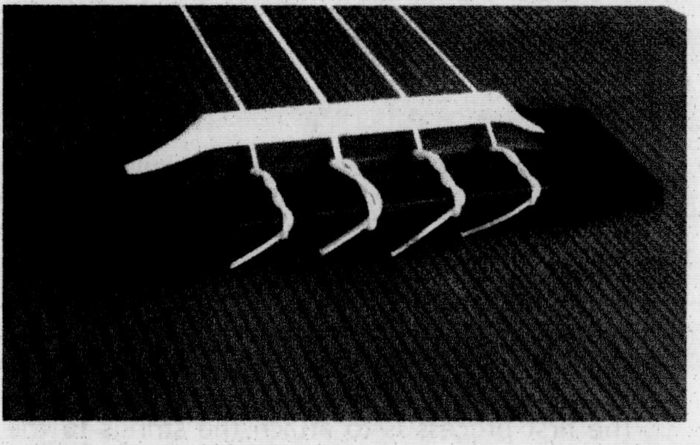

TECHNICAL INFORMATION

METRIC TO IMPERIAL CONVERSIONS

MM	.000"	Fractions	MM	.000"	Fractions	MM	.000"	Fractions
0.79	0.031	1/32"	15.00	0.591		30.16	1.187	1-3/16"
1.00	0.039		15.08	0.594	19/32"	31.00	1.220	
1.59	0.062	1/16"	15.88	0.625	5/8"	31.75	1.250	1-1/4"
2.00	0.079		16.00	0.630		32.00	1.260	
2.38	0.094	3/32"	16.67	0.656	21/32"	33.00	1.299	
3.00	0.118		17.00	0.669		33.34	1.313	1-5/16"
3.18	0.125	1/8"	17.46	0.688	11/16"	34.00	1.339	
3.97	0.156	5/32"	18.00	0.709		34.93	1.375	1-3/8"
4.00	0.157		18.26	0.719	23/32"	35.00	1.378	
4.76	0.188	3/16"	19.00	0.748		36.00	1.417	
5.00	0.197		19.05	0.750	3/4"	36.51	1.437	1-7/16"
5.56	0.219	7/32"	19.84	0.781	25/32"	37.00	1.457	
6.00	0.236		20.00	0.787		38.00	1.496	
6.35	0.250	1/4"	20.64	0.813	13/16"	38.10	1.500	1-1/2"
7.00	0.276		21.00	0.827		39.00	1.535	
7.14	0.281	9/32"	21.43	0.844	27/32"	39.69	1.563	1-9/16"
7.94	0.313	5/16"	22.00	0.866		40.00	1.575	
8.00	0.315		22.23	0.875	7/8"	41.00	1.614	
8.73	0.344	11/32"	23.00	0.906		41.28	1.625	1-5/8"
9.00	0.354		23.02	0.906	29/32"	42.00	1.654	
9.53	0.375	3/8"	23.81	0.938	15/16"	42.86	1.687	1-11/16"
10.00	0.394		24.00	0.945		43.00	1.693	
10.32	0.406	13/32"	24.61	0.969	31/32"	44.00	1.732	
11.00	0.433		25.00	0.984		44.45	1.750	1-3/4"
11.11	0.438	7/16"	25.40	1.000	1"	45.00	1.772	
11.91	0.469	15/32"	26.00	1.024		46.00	1.811	
12.00	0.472		26.99	1.063	1-1/16"	46.04	1.813	1-13/16"
12.70	0.500	1/2"	27.00	1.063		47.00	1.850	
13.00	0.512		28.00	1.102		47.63	1.875	1-7/8"
13.49	0.531	17/32"	28.58	1.125	1-1/8"	48.00	1.890	
14.00	0.551		29.00	1.142		49.00	1.929	
14.29	0.563	9/16"	30.00	1.181		49.21	1.937	1-15/16"

METRIC TO IMPERIAL CONVERSIONS

MM	.000"	Fractions	MM	.000"	Fractions	MM	.000"	Fractions
50.00	1.969		115.00	4.528		228.60	9.000	9"
50.80	2.000	2"	120.00	4.724		230.00	9.055	
53.98	2.125	2-1/8"	120.65	4.750	4-3/4"	240.00	9.449	
55.00	2.165		125.00	4.921		241.30	9.500	9-1/2"
57.15	2.250	2-1/4"	127.00	5.000	5"	250.00	9.843	
60.00	2.362		130.00	5.118		254.00	10.000	10"
60.33	2.375	2-3/8"	133.35	5.250	5-1/4"	260.00	10.236	
63.50	2.500	2-1/2"	135.00	5.315		270.00	10.630	
65.00	2.559		139.70	5.500	5-1/2"	279.40	11.000	11"
66.68	2.625	2-5/8"	140.00	5.512		280.00	11.024	
69.85	2.750	2-3/4"	145.00	5.709		290.00	11.417	
70.00	2.756		146.05	5.750	5-3/4"	300.00	11.811	
73.03	2.875	2-7/8"	150.00	5.906		304.80	12.000	12"
75.00	2.953		152.40	6.000	6"	330.20	13.000	13"
76.20	3.000	3"	158.75	6.250	6-1/4"	355.60	14.000	14"
80.00	3.150		160.00	6.299		381.00	15.000	15"
82.55	3.250	3-1/4"	165.10	6.500	6-1/2"	406.40	16.000	16"
85.00	3.346		170.00	6.693		431.80	17.000	17"
88.90	3.500	3-1/2"	171.45	6.750	6-3/4"	457.20	18.000	18"
90.00	3.543		177.80	7.000	7"	482.60	19.000	19"
95.00	3.740		180.00	7.087		508.00	20.000	20"
95.25	3.750	3-3/4"	190.00	7.480		533.40	21.000	21"
100.00	3.937		190.50	7.500	7-1/2"	558.80	22.000	22"
101.60	4.000	4"	200.00	7.874		584.20	23.000	23"
105.00	4.134		203.20	8.000	8"	609.60	24.000	24"
107.95	4.250	4-1/4"	210.00	8.268		635.00	25.000	25"
110.00	4.331		215.90	8.500	8-1/2"	660.40	26.000	26"
114.30	4.500	4-1/2"	220.00	8.661		685.80	27.000	27"

PITCHES & FREQUENCIES FOR AN EQUAL-TEMPERED SCALE

A4 = 440Hz Middle C is C4

Note									
	0	1	2	3	4	5	6	7	
C	16.35Hz	32.70	65.41	130.81	261.63	523.25	1046.50	2093.00	C
C#/Db	17.32	34.65	69.30	138.59	277.18	554.37	1108.73	2217.46	C#/Db
D	18.35	36.71	73.42	146.83	293.66	587.33	1174.66	2349.32	D
D#/Eb	19.45	38.89	77.78	155.56	311.13	622.25	1244.51	2489.02	D#/Eb
E	20.60	41.20	82.41	164.81	329.63	659.26	1318.51	2637.02	E
F	21.83	43.65	87.31	174.61	349.23	698.46	1396.91	2793.83	F
F#/Gb	23.12	46.25	92.50	185.00	369.99	739.99	1479.98	2959.96	F#/Gb
G	24.50	49.00	98.00	196.00	392.00	783.99	1567.98	3135.96	G
G#/Ab	25.96	51.91	103.83	207.65	415.30	830.61	1661.22	3322.44	G#/Ab
A	27.50	55.00	110.00	220.00	440.00	880.00	1760.00	3520.00	A
A#/Bb	29.14	58.27	116.54	233.08	466.16	932.33	1864.66	3729.31	A#/Bb
B	30.87	61.74	123.47	246.94	493.88	987.77	1975.53	3951.07	B
C	32.70	65.41	130.81	261.63	523.25	1046.50	2093.00	4186.01	C

The octave numbers in the chart above are American Standard Scientific Pitch Notation. Middle C is C4 using this notation and standard ukulele tuning is **G4-C4-E4-A4**. An alternative notation is Helmholtz Notation where the octaves are shown by commas or apostrophes. Ukulele tuning is then written as **g'-c'-e'-a'**. The strings of a ukulele will vibrate at 392Hz, 261.63Hz, 329.63Hz and 440Hz.

FRET POSITIONS - RULE OF 18

SOPRANO 343MM/13.5"

		remainder	from nut
Fret 1	19.06	323.94	19.06
Fret 2	18.00	305.95	37.05
Fret 3	17.00	288.95	54.05
Fret 4	16.05	272.90	70.10
Fret 5	15.16	257.74	85.26
Fret 6	14.32	243.42	99.58
Fret 7	13.52	229.89	113.11
Fret 8	12.77	217.12	125.88
Fret 9	12.06	205.06	137.94
Fret 10	11.39	193.67	149.33
Fret 11	10.76	182.91	160.09
Fret 12	10.16	172.75	170.25
Fret 13	9.60	163.15	179.85
Fret 14	9.06	154.09	188.91
Fret 15	8.56	145.53	197.47
Fret 16	8.08	137.44	205.56
Fret17	7.64	129.81	213.19
Fret 18	7.21	122.59	220.41
Fret 19	6.81	115.78	227.22
Fret 20	6.43	109.35	233.65
Fret 21	6.08	103.28	239.72
Fret 22	5.74	97.54	245.46
Fret 23	5.42	92.12	250.88
Fret 24	5.12	87.00	256.00

CONCERT 381MM/15"

		remainder	from nut
Fret 1	21.17	359.83	21.17
Fret 2	19.99	339.84	41.16
Fret 3	18.88	320.96	60.04
Fret 4	17.83	303.13	77.87
Fret 5	16.84	286.29	94.71
Fret 6	15.91	270.39	110.61
Fret 7	15.02	255.36	125.64
Fret 8	14.19	241.18	139.82
Fret 9	13.40	227.78	153.22
Fret 10	12.65	215.12	165.88
Fret 11	11.95	203.17	177.83
Fret 12	11.29	191.89	189.11
Fret 13	10.66	181.23	199.77
Fret 14	10.07	171.16	209.84
Fret 15	9.51	161.65	219.35
Fret 16	8.98	152.67	228.33
Fret17	8.48	144.19	236.81
Fret 18	8.01	136.18	244.82
Fret 19	7.57	128.61	252.39
Fret 20	7.15	121.47	259.53
Fret 21	6.75	114.72	266.28
Fret 22	6.37	108.34	272.66
Fret 23	6.02	102.33	278.67
Fret 24	5.68	96.64	284.36

FRET POSITIONS - RULE OF 18

TENOR 432MM/17"

		remainder	from nut
Fret 1	24.00	408.00	24.00
Fret 2	22.67	385.33	46.67
Fret 3	21.41	363.93	68.07
Fret 4	20.22	343.71	88.29
Fret 5	19.09	324.61	107.39
Fret 6	18.03	306.58	125.42
Fret 7	17.03	289.55	142.45
Fret 8	16.09	273.46	158.54
Fret 9	15.19	258.27	173.73
Fret 10	14.35	243.92	188.08
Fret 11	13.55	230.37	201.63
Fret 12	12.80	217.57	214.43
Fret 13	12.09	205.48	226.52
Fret 14	11.42	194.07	237.93
Fret 15	10.78	183.29	248.71
Fret 16	10.18	173.10	258.90
Fret17	9.62	163.49	268.51
Fret 18	9.08	154.40	277.60
Fret 19	8.58	145.83	286.17
Fret 20	8.10	137.72	294.28
Fret 21	7.65	130.07	301.93
Fret 22	7.23	122.85	309.15
Fret 23	6.82	116.02	315.98
Fret 24	6.45	109.58	322.42

BARITONE 508MM/20"

		remainder	from nut
Fret 1	28.22	479.78	28.22
Fret 2	26.65	453.12	54.88
Fret 3	25.17	427.95	80.05
Fret 4	23.77	404.17	103.83
Fret 5	22.45	381.72	126.28
Fret 6	21.21	360.51	147.49
Fret 7	20.03	340.49	167.51
Fret 8	18.92	321.57	186.43
Fret 9	17.86	303.70	204.30
Fret 10	16.87	286.83	221.17
Fret 11	15.94	270.90	237.10
Fret 12	15.05	255.85	252.15
Fret 13	14.21	241.63	266.37
Fret 14	13.42	228.21	279.79
Fret 15	12.68	215.53	292.47
Fret 16	11.97	203.56	304.44
Fret17	11.31	192.25	315.75
Fret 18	10.68	181.57	326.43
Fret 19	10.09	171.48	336.52
Fret 20	9.53	161.95	346.05
Fret 21	9.00	152.96	355.04
Fret 22	8.50	144.46	363.54
Fret 23	8.03	136.43	371.57
Fret 24	7.58	128.85	379.15

Note: If the fret slots are to be cut with a template using either a hand- or table saw, a tenor ukulele template can be used for concert and soprano fretboards, starting at the second and fourth fret positions respectively. This will result in slightly different scale lengths than the calculations on the previous page, but it makes little or no difference on the finished instrument. The length of the neck will have to be adjusted slightly as well as the placement of the bridge.

Similarly a template machined to a baritone scale length can accomodate all four scales, starting the tenor at the third fret, the concert at the fifth and the soprano at the seventh fret. Such a template will need to have enough marked fret positions to cope with the soprano fretboard.

FRET POSITIONS - 17.817

SOPRANO 343MM/13.5"

		remainder	from nut
Fret 1	19.25	323.75	19.25
Fret 2	18.17	305.58	37.42
Fret 3	17.15	288.43	54.57
Fret 4	16.19	272.24	70.76
Fret 5	15.28	256.96	86.04
Fret 6	14.42	242.54	100.46
Fret 7	13.61	228.92	114.08
Fret 8	12.85	216.08	126.92
Fret 9	12.13	203.95	139.05
Fret 10	11.45	192.50	150.50
Fret 11	10.80	181.70	161.30
Fret 12	10.20	171.50	171.50
Fret 13	9.63	161.87	181.13
Fret 14	9.09	152.79	190.21
Fret 15	8.58	144.21	198.79
Fret 16	8.09	136.12	206.88
Fret17	7.64	128.48	214.52
Fret 18	7.21	121.27	221.73
Fret 19	6.81	114.46	228.54
Fret 20	6.42	108.04	234.96
Fret 21	6.06	101.97	241.03
Fret 22	5.72	96.25	246.75
Fret 23	5.40	90.85	252.15
Fret 24	5.10	85.75	257.25

CONCERT 381MM/15"

		remainder	from nut
Fret 1	21.38	359.62	21.38
Fret 2	20.18	339.43	41.57
Fret 3	19.05	320.38	60.62
Fret 4	17.98	302.40	78.60
Fret 5	16.97	285.43	95.57
Fret 6	16.02	269.41	111.59
Fret 7	15.12	254.29	126.71
Fret 8	14.27	240.01	140.99
Fret 9	13.47	226.54	154.46
Fret 10	12.71	213.83	167.17
Fret 11	12.00	201.83	179.17
Fret 12	11.33	190.50	190.50
Fret 13	10.69	179.81	201.19
Fret 14	10.09	169.71	211.29
Fret 15	9.53	160.19	220.81
Fret 16	8.99	151.20	229.80
Fret17	8.49	142.71	238.29
Fret 18	8.01	134.70	246.30
Fret 19	7.56	127.14	253.86
Fret 20	7.14	120.01	260.99
Fret 21	6.74	113.27	267.73
Fret 22	6.36	106.91	274.09
Fret 23	6.00	100.91	280.09
Fret 24	5.66	95.25	285.75

FRET POSITIONS - 17.817

TENOR 432MM/17"

		remainder	from nut
Fret 1	24.25	407.75	24.25
Fret 2	22.89	384.87	47.13
Fret 3	21.60	363.27	68.73
Fret 4	20.39	342.88	89.12
Fret 5	19.24	323.63	108.37
Fret 6	18.16	305.47	126.53
Fret 7	17.14	288.32	143.68
Fret 8	16.18	272.14	159.86
Fret 9	15.27	256.87	175.13
Fret 10	14.42	242.45	189.55
Fret 11	13.61	228.84	203.16
Fret 12	12.84	216.00	216.00
Fret 13	12.12	203.88	228.12
Fret 14	11.44	192.43	239.57
Fret 15	10.80	181.63	250.37
Fret 16	10.19	171.44	260.56
Fret17	9.62	161.82	270.18
Fret 18	9.08	152.73	279.27
Fret 19	8.57	144.16	287.84
Fret 20	8.09	136.07	295.93
Fret 21	7.64	128.43	303.57
Fret 22	7.21	121.22	310.78
Fret 23	6.80	114.42	317.58
Fret 24	6.42	108.00	324.00

BARITONE 508MM/20"

		remainder	from nut
Fret 1	28.51	479.49	28.51
Fret 2	26.91	452.58	55.42
Fret 3	25.40	427.17	80.83
Fret 4	23.98	403.20	104.80
Fret 5	22.63	380.57	127.43
Fret 6	21.36	359.21	148.79
Fret 7	20.16	339.05	168.95
Fret 8	19.03	320.02	187.98
Fret 9	17.96	302.06	205.94
Fret 10	16.95	285.10	222.90
Fret 11	16.00	269.10	238.90
Fret 12	15.10	254.00	254.00
Fret 13	14.26	239.74	268.26
Fret 14	13.46	226.29	281.71
Fret 15	12.70	213.59	294.41
Fret 16	11.99	201.60	306.40
Fret17	11.31	190.28	317.72
Fret 18	10.68	179.60	328.40
Fret 19	10.08	169.52	338.48
Fret 20	9.51	160.01	347.99
Fret 21	8.98	151.03	356.97
Fret 22	8.48	142.55	365.45
Fret 23	8.00	134.55	373.45
Fret 24	7.55	127.00	381.00

Note: If the fret slots are to be cut with a template using either a hand- or table saw, a tenor ukulele template can be used for concert and soprano fretboards, starting at the second and fourth fret positions respectively. This will result in slightly different scale lengths than the calculations on the previous page, but it makes little or no difference on the finished instrument. The length of the neck will have to be adjusted slightly as well as the placement of the bridge.

Similarly a template machined to a baritone scale length can accomodate all four scales, starting the tenor at the third fret, the concert at the fifth and the soprano at the seventh fret.

Compensation of 2mm should be added to the theorectical scale length when placing the bridge when the frets are calculated using 17.817 as the devisor.

A GLOSSARY OF THE UKULELE

action - the height of the strings above the frets, usually measured at the 12th fret.
back - The part of the ukulele that rests on the player's body, usually a thin piece of timber with one or more re-enforcing *braces*.
binding - narrow strips of wood or plastic glued into a ledge cut into the edges of the body (and sometimes the fretboard) to protect the edges and add decoration.
bolt-on - a neck which is attached to the body by mechanical means.
bout - the curved upper and lower parts of the body of the ukulele, separated by the *waist*.
bracing - small pieces of timber, usually softwood, glued on the inside of the soundboard and back to add rigidity and control resonances.
bridge - a piece of hardwood glued to the soundboard which transfers the strings' vibrations to the body through the *saddle*.
bridge pins - small tapered pins used to anchor the strings to the *bridge*.
bridge plate - a thin strip of timber glued to the inside of the soundboard under the bridge.
compensation - a 2mm addition to the string length added to compensate for the slight sharpening of the strings when pushed down to the fretboard.
fretboard, fingerboard - a piece of hardwood glued to the face of the neck into which *frets* are inserted into pre-cut slots.
frets - metal strips inset in the fretboard to stop the strings' vibration.
fret marker - a piece of plastic or shell inlaid into the fretboard to visually identify fret positions.
head, headstock, peghead - the flat extension of the neck into which the tuning machines are mounted.
heel - the end of the neck where it joins the body
intonation - the ability of the instrument to play in tune, dependant on the correct placement of the frets and bridge.
ivoroid - a celluloid plastic that imitates ivory, often used for binding.
lining - strips of wood used to strengthen the join between the sides, soundboard and back. These can be solid, pre-bent to the shape of the sides, or kerfed with regular slots cut almost the whole way through to allow the strip to follow the curve of the sides while being glued.
neck - the wooden arm underneath the *fretboard* that connects the body to the head and allows the strings to be fretted.
neckblock - a wooden block inside the body to which the soundboard, sides and back are glued, as well as being the anchoring point for a *bolt-on* neck.
nut - a piece of bone, hardwood or synthetic material at the end of the fretboard which sets the string spacing and height of the strings above the fretboard.
pin bridge - a bridge which uses *bridge pins* to anchor the strings under the bridge, most commonly used on steel string acoustic guitars.
pin-less bridge - a bridge where the strings are tied to the bridge or otherwise anchored to the back or underneath of the bridge.
purfling - decorative strips of timber veneer or plastic glued inside the *binding*.
rosette - decorative re-enforcement inlaid into the soundboard around the *soundhole*.
saddle - a piece of bone, hardwood or synthetic material set into a slot in the bridge at the end of the predetermined string length.
scale length, string length - the vibrating length of the strings.
sides, ribs - thin pieces of timber bent to shape by heat to form the outline of the body.
soundboard, top, face, table - the vibrating surface of the ukulele, stimulated by the strings through the bridge. It can be made of hardwood or softwood.
soundhole - a hole cut in the soundboard to assist in sound production.
tail block - a wooden block at the end of the body to which the sides, soundboard and back are glued.
tentallones - small triangular blocks of wood used to glue together the soundboard and the sides.
tuning machines, machine heads - geared mechanical fittings to adjust string tension and tune the instrument.
tuning pegs - un-geared friction pegs used to tune a ukulele.

PICKUPS & ELECTRONICS

Piezo pickups are commonly fitted to many ukuleles for stage performance. Piezo ceramic crystals produce an electrical current when flexed and this can be fed into an amplifier and speakers. Piezos are commonly used in a couple of different ways.

A thin layer of the material is applied to a small copper disk which can be glued to the inside of a ukulele soundboard with electrical connections to the copper backing and the piezo ceramic. The conducting wires are attached to a standard ¼″ output socket, usually fitted to the tailblock. The socket can also act as a strap pin. There are several commercially available brands such as K&K and Schertler. For the more adventurous, piezo disks of several sizes are available and are commonly used in the cigar-box guitar community to amplify those instruments.

The other approach is to enclose a strip of piezo inside a tube of flexible braided copper wire, in the manner of a co-axial cable. This is fitted underneath the saddle and compressed by string tension. A small diameter co-axial cable is attached to the end of the piezo section and connected to an output socket, again usually fitted through the tailblock.

These pickups can be plugged straight into a PA amplifier but will sound thin and with a harsh tonal quality referred to as 'piezo quack'. This is due to a mismatch of electrical impedance. A buffering pre-amplifier is needed to match the impedance of the pickup to that of the amplifier.

Some under-saddle pickups come with a small, battery-powered pre-amplifier (*pre-amp*) mounted on the output socket, but these do tend to be at the upper end of the market. Others have the pre-amp and control knobs (and sometimes even an electronic tuner) mounted in a unit which can fit into a hole cut into the side of the ukulele. This can be an advantage for an instrument used mainly for performing on stage, but many people do not want to cut a hole in the side of their ukulele.

Alternatively the pre-amp can be an outboard unit similar to a guitar effects pedal. This means that the only thing on the instrument itself is the pickup and an output socket.

The cost of a pickup with a pre-amp can range from a few dollars up to several hundred. The cheaper ones are available by mail from China and are cheap enough to allow experimentation at little cost. There are many on-line communities who discuss such things and information is freely available.

This is a list of people that I have dealt with in the past, or have been recommended by other people. For the Australian and European suppliers I have given the number that needs to be dialled from overseas (with the addition of whatever numbers are needed to make an international call).

TOOLS AND SUPPLIES

Stewart-MacDonald's Guitar Shop Supply
21 N. Shafer St. or P.O. Box 900, Athens, OH 45701 USA
Ph: 800 848 2273
Fax: 740 593 7922
www.stewmac.com
Free comprehensive catalog, tools and jigs, parts, binding materials, inlay materials, finishing supplies, neck and body blanks, wood, instrument kits, instruction videos, books.

Luthiers Mercantile International, Inc.
7975 Cameron Dr. Bldg. 1600 Windsor, CA 95492, California, USA
www.lmii.com
Free catalog, tools and jigs, parts, binding materials, inlay materials, finishing supplies, neck and body blanks, wood, instrument kits, instruction videos, books.

Allied Lutherie Ltd.
POB 217, 498 A Moore Lane,
Healdsburg, CA 95448 USA
Ph: 707 431 3760
Fax: 707 431 3762
www.alliedlutherie.com
Timber, parts & tools.

Guitarwoods - Darrell Wheeler Custom Guitars
Unit 5 / 6-10 Booralee Street,
Botany NSW Australia 2019
Ph: +612 9316 7467
www.guitarwoods.com.au
Timber, parts & tools.

Scott Wise, Wise Luthiers
27 Elizabeth St, Margaret River, WA, Australia 6285
www.scottwise.net
Wood.

Australian Luthier Supplies
Hancock Guitars, PO Box 17, Eagle Heights, Qld 4271 Australia
Ph. +614 0963 5288
www.luthierssupplies.com.au
Timber, parts.

Hana Lima 'la - Michael Chock
718 Pu'uhale Rd, Honolulu, HA 96819
Ph. 808 847 1541
www.hanalima.com
Timber, parts, kits & instructional materials.

David Dyke's Luthiers Supplies
The Hall, Horebeech Lane, Horam,
Heathfield, East Sussex, TN21 0HR, England
Ph: +44 1435 812315
www.luthierssupplies.co.uk
Timber, parts & tools.

Touchstone Tonewoods Ltd.
44 Albert Road North, Reigate,
Surrey, RH2 9EZ, England
Ph: +44 1737 221064
www.touchstonetonewoods.co.uk
Timber, parts & tools.

DICK - Qualitätsprodukte für Musikinstrumente
Donaustraße 51, D-94523 Metten, Germany
Ph: +49 991 91099
www.dick-gmbh.de
Downloadable pdf catalogs with a wide range of tools.

Axiom Inc. - Bill James
5350 Pioneer Creek Dr., Suite # 4
P.O. Box 457, Maple Plain, MN 55359 USA
www.axinc.net
Celluloid binding.

Luthier Suppliers
7605 E. Kenyon Ave. Denver, CO 80237 USA
Ph: 720 256 8470
http://www.luthiersuppliers.com
Specialised tools.

FURTHER READING AND WEB SURFING

Michael Chock, *'Ukulele Construction Manual*, Hana Lima 'la, 2004

Bill Plant, *Make Your Own Ukulele*, Fox Chapel Publishing, 2012

Sarah Greenbaum & John Weissenrieder, *The Uke Book Illustrated*, Fox Chapel Publishing, 2019

Making a Ukulele- The Ford Motor Company, 1917 (https://www.youtube.com/watch?v=MxapCiRm278)

American Lutherie - the quarterly journal published by the Guild of American Luthiers (www.luth.org) since 1984 is an invaluable resource of information.

Guitarmaker - the quarterly journal of the Association of Stringed Instrument Artisans (www. guitarmaker.org) is an equally valuable resource.

The Fretboard Journal - a quarterly magazine devoted to fretted instruments (www.fretboardjournal.com).

Ukulele Magazine - a quarterly magazine devoted, naturally enough, to ukuleles (www.ukulelemag.com).

The University of NSW pages on musical instrument acoustics (newt.phys.unsw.edu.au/jw/basics.html).

Ukulele Underground (www.ukuleleunderground.com) is an on-line discussion forum covering all aspects of ukulele building, playing and ownership.

There are numerous other on-line discussion groups on instrument building. Most concentrate on guitars, but can be great sources of information on tools, jigs and sources of materials.

Full sized drawings of all five ukuleles to accompany the book are available at www.mcdonaldstrings.com/ukebook/ukuleleplans.pdf